VIETNAM

TRAVEL GUIDE 2025 AND BEYOND

A Journey Through Culture, Hidden Gems, Cuisine and Local Secrets in Southeast Asia on the Eastern edge of the Peninsula – Packed with Detailed Maps & Itinerary Planner

BY

JAMES W. PATRICK

Copyright © 2024 by James W. Patrick. All rights reserved. The content of this work, including but not limited to text, images, and other media, is owned by James W. Patrick and is protected under copyright laws and international agreements. No part of this work may be reproduced, shared, or transmitted in any form or by any means without the explicit written consent of James W. Patrick. Unauthorized use, duplication, or distribution of this material may lead to legal action, including both civil and criminal penalties. For permission requests or further inquiries, please reach out to the author via the contact details provided in the book or on the author's official page.

TABLE OF CONTENTS

Chapter 1. Introduction.. 6

1.1 Welcome to Vietnam... 6

1.2 My Experience in Vietnam...7

1.3 About This Guide...9

Chapter 2. Getting Started...12

2.1 Understanding Vietnam..12

2.2 Geography, Climate & Best Time to Visit...............................14

2.3 History and Culture... 16

2.4 Cultural Do's and Don'ts...17

2.5 Language, Communication & Essential Vietnamese Phrases..... 19

2.6 Currency and Money Matters...22

Chapter 3. Planning Your Trip... 25

3.1 Visa and Entry Requirements...25

3.2 Packing Essentials... 27

3.3 Budgeting for Your Trip..28

3.4 Accommodation Options..30

3.5 Transportation Options..33

Chapter 4. Exploring Hanoi... 36

4.1 Overview of Hanoi... 36

4.2 Must-See Attractions..39

4.2.1 Old Quarter...40

4.2.2 Ho Chi Minh Mausoleum..43

4.2.3 Temple of Literature...46

4.2.4 Ha Long Bay...48

4.3 Hidden Gems of Hanoi..50

4.4 Exploring Hanoi's Neighborhoods..53

4.5 Dining and Nightlife in Hanoi...55

Chapter 5. Discovering Northern Vietnam.................................59

5.1 Overview of Northern Vietnam.................................59

5.2 Must-See Attractions.................................63

5.2.1 Sapa Town.................................64

5.2.2 Bac Ha Market.................................67

5.2.3 Ha Giang Province.................................70

5.2.4 Ninh Binh Province.................................73

5.3 Hidden Gems of Northern Vietnam.................................76

5.4 Trekking and Homestays.................................79

Chapter 6. Exploring Central Vietnam.................................82

6.1 Overview of Central Vietnam.................................82

6.2 Must-See Attractions.................................85

6.2.1 Hue Imperial City.................................86

6.2.2 Hoi An Ancient Town.................................89

6.2.3 Da Nang City.................................92

6.2.4 My Son Sanctuary.................................96

6.3 Hidden Gems of Central Vietnam.................................98

6.4 Beaches and Water Activities.................................100

Chapter 7. Discovering Southern Vietnam.................................103

7.1 Overview of Southern Vietnam.................................103

7.2 Must-See Attractions.................................106

7.2.1 Ho Chi Minh City.................................107

7.2.2 Mekong Delta.................................110

7.2.3 Cu Chi Tunnels.................................112

7.2.4 Can Tho City.................................115

7.3 Hidden Gems of Southern Vietnam.................................118

7.4 Floating Markets and Village Life.................................119

Chapter 8. Exploring Vietnam's Islands.................................122

8.1 Overview of Vietnam's Islands.................................122

8.2 Must-See Attractions..124

8.2.1 Phu Quoc Island..124

8.2.2 Con Dao Islands..127

8.2.3 Cat Ba Island..129

8.2.4 Ly Son Island..132

8.3 Hidden Gems of Vietnam's Islands................................135

Chapter 9. Discovering Vietnamese Cuisine..........................136

9.1 Overview of Vietnamese Cuisine................................136

9.2 Must-Try Dishes..138

9.2.1 Pho..138

9.2.2 Banh Mi..139

9.2.3 Goi Cuon..141

9.2.4 Bun Cha..142

9.3 Hidden Gems of Vietnamese Cuisine............................143

9.4 Cooking Classes and Food Tours................................145

Chapter 10. Immersing in Vietnamese Culture.......................148

10.1 Festivals and Events..148

10.2 Vietnamese Folk Traditions................................150

10.3 Arts and Music Scene..153

10.4 Vietnamese Coffee Culture................................155

Chapter 11. Outdoor Adventures................................158

11.1 Hiking Trails and Nature Walks................................158

11.2 Cycling Routes..159

11.3 Water Activities: Kayaking, Rafting, and Fishing...............161

11.4 Winter Sports: Surfing and Rock Climbing......................163

11.5 Wildlife Watching: Birds and Animals.........................165

Chapter 12. Practical Information and Travel Resources.............168

12.1 Maps of Vietnam: Hanoi, Ho Chi Minh City, and Key Destinations........169

12.2 Five Days Itinerary..170

12.3 Safety Tips and Emergency Contacts................................171

12.4 Shopping and Souvenirs..173

12.5 Useful Websites, Mobile Apps, and Online Resources................175

12.6 Internet Access and Connectivity................................177

12.7 Visitor Centers and Tourist Assistance...........................179

Conclusion and Recommendations.......................................180

CHAPTER 1
INTRODUCTION

1.1 Welcome to Vietnam

Welcome to Vietnam, a Southeast Asian country brimming with a rich tapestry of history, culture, and natural beauty. Situated on the eastern edge of the Indochinese Peninsula, Vietnam is bordered by China to the north, Laos and Cambodia to the west, and the South China Sea to the east and south. Its geography ranges from the bustling cities along the coast to lush forests, serene rice terraces, and impressive mountain ranges inland. Whether you're drawn to the country's urban energy or its tranquil countryside, Vietnam offers an adventure that appeals to all kinds of travelers. For those visiting Vietnam for the first time, one of the first things to note is its vibrant cities, especially Hanoi in the north and Ho Chi Minh City in the south. Hanoi, the capital, offers a glimpse into the country's past with its colonial architecture, traditional temples, and Old Quarter streets filled with shops and markets. Ho Chi Minh City, formerly known as Saigon, is a hub of modern life, where skyscrapers tower over French-influenced buildings, and the streets pulse with energy from motorbikes, street vendors, and cafes. Both cities are excellent starting points for exploring the cultural fabric of the nation. Travelers should also be aware that Vietnam has a tropical climate, with varying weather conditions depending on the region and time of year. In the north, expect cooler winters, while the south remains hot and humid throughout the year. Planning your trip around the weather is essential, especially if you intend to explore the famous beaches along the coast or embark on trekking adventures in the northern mountains.

One of the highlights of Vietnam is its cuisine, a harmonious blend of flavors that draws from fresh herbs, rice, seafood, and meats. Street food culture thrives here, offering visitors the chance to taste local dishes like pho, banh mi, and spring rolls. Eating from local vendors is a great way to experience authentic flavors, and it's both delicious and affordable. Vietnam's transportation system is well-developed, though navigating it may take some getting used to. Domestic flights connect major cities, while buses and trains offer scenic routes through the countryside. For shorter distances, motorbike rentals are popular, though travelers should exercise caution and consider their comfort level with Vietnam's often chaotic traffic. Vietnamese people are known for their hospitality, and despite language barriers, many locals go out of their way to make visitors feel welcome. Learning a few basic Vietnamese phrases can go a long way in enhancing your experience. The currency used is the Vietnamese dong, and while major cities are equipped with ATMs and card payment systems, carrying cash is recommended when traveling to more rural areas. From the ancient town of Hoi An, known for its lantern-lit nights and tailor shops, to the majestic limestone cliffs of Ha Long Bay, Vietnam is a country that captures the heart of every visitor. It is a destination that requires both an open mind and a willingness to immerse oneself in its dynamic culture. Whether you are exploring ancient pagodas, soaking up the local history, or simply enjoying the breathtaking natural landscapes, Vietnam offers a journey unlike any other, with unforgettable memories waiting at every turn.

1.2 My Experience in Vietnam

My experience in Vietnam was nothing short of transformative. From the moment I set foot in this mesmerizing country, I felt like I had entered a completely different world—one where every corner seemed to offer a new discovery, a fresh perspective, and a chance to connect with something deeply human and real. It wasn't just the landscapes, the bustling cities, or even the delicious food that made it unforgettable; it was the feeling of immersion in a culture so rich, layered, and alive.

I landed in Hanoi, Vietnam's capital, not knowing exactly what to expect. I'd read about the old-world charm of the city, its mix of French colonial architecture and traditional Vietnamese influences. But no guidebook could have prepared me for the soul of the place. As I wandered through the narrow, lively streets of the Old Quarter, I was immediately drawn in by the vibrant energy. Motorbikes whizzed past, the scent of street food filled the air, and everywhere I looked, there was something happening—vendors selling fresh fruit, people sitting on tiny stools, sipping coffee, and old men playing chess by the roadside. There was a rhythm to the chaos, a harmony in the hustle and bustle, and it was in that very chaos that I found the pulse of Vietnam. One evening, I sat by Hoan Kiem Lake, a peaceful oasis in the heart of the city. Watching the locals practice tai chi at sunrise and couples strolling hand in hand under the soft glow of lanterns made me realize how deeply intertwined the people of Vietnam are with their history and traditions. It's a country that doesn't just remember its past—it lives it, breathes it, and carries it forward in every interaction, every smile, every gesture of kindness. This connection to heritage is felt everywhere, from the ancient temples that dot the landscape to the stories shared by the elderly over tea. After a few days in Hanoi, I took a trip to Ha Long Bay, one of the natural wonders of the world. As our boat sailed between the towering limestone karsts rising dramatically from the emerald waters, I couldn't help but feel humbled by the sheer beauty of the place. It was as if time had stood still there—untouched, pure, and almost surreal. We kayaked through hidden caves and swam in the tranquil waters, completely lost in the serenity of it all. I remember standing on the deck of the boat that evening, watching the sun dip below the horizon, casting a golden glow over the bay. In that moment, I felt a deep sense of peace, a connection to something far greater than myself.

Vietnam, however, isn't just about breathtaking landscapes. It's about the warmth of its people. From Hanoi, I journeyed south to Hoi An, a charming, ancient town famous for its lantern-lit nights and tailor shops. The people of Hoi An welcomed me as if I were an old friend. I spent my days cycling through rice paddies, visiting local artisans, and, of course, getting custom-made clothes from the town's skilled tailors. But what struck me most was the kindness of the locals. One afternoon, after a sudden downpour had drenched me to the bone, an elderly woman invited me into her small home for tea. We didn't share a common language, but we shared smiles, gestures, and a simple, warm moment that will stay with me forever. In Ho Chi Minh City, the energy was different—more fast-paced, modern, and dynamic. Yet even here, amidst the skyscrapers and rush of daily life, I found pockets of serenity. A visit to the Cu Chi Tunnels brought me face-to-face with Vietnam's resilient spirit. Crawling through those narrow, dark tunnels where soldiers once fought, I gained a profound respect for the history of struggle and triumph that shaped the nation. Throughout my journey, one constant remained: the food. From the rich, hearty bowls of pho to the crispy banh mi sandwiches, every meal was an experience, bursting with flavors that reflected the diversity of Vietnam's regions. I found myself eating street food most of the time, enjoying the incredible variety of dishes prepared fresh right in front of me, each one telling a story of its own. Vietnam changed me. It's not just a place to visit, it's a place to feel. The mix of natural beauty, history, and warm, welcoming people left an indelible mark on my heart. I left with memories, friendships, and a deep sense of gratitude. If there is one destination that will surprise, inspire, and humble you, it is Vietnam. I cannot wait to return, and I know that once you experience it for yourself, you'll feel the same pull to come back, time and time again.

1.3 About This Guide

This Vietnam Travel Guide 2025 and Beyond is your ultimate companion to discovering the wonders of this vibrant Southeast Asian nation. Designed to offer travelers a comprehensive and immersive experience, this guide provides all the essential information needed for a successful and unforgettable trip. From practical tips on navigating the country's cities to insights into its rich cultural heritage, this guide ensures that every aspect of your journey is covered with care and detail.

Maps and Navigation

Maps and navigation are crucial when exploring Vietnam's diverse landscapes. This guide offers both digital and offline maps to help travelers easily find their way. Whether you're navigating the bustling streets of Hanoi or trekking in the mountains of Sapa, you'll have access to detailed routes and directions at your fingertips.

Geography and climates

When it comes to planning your trip, the guide breaks down the best times to visit Vietnam, depending on the region and weather patterns. It helps you decide when to travel based on festivals, climate, and personal preferences. Additionally, it provides advice on visa requirements, travel insurance, and health precautions to ensure a smooth journey.

Accommodation options

Accommodation options are plentiful in Vietnam, ranging from luxury resorts to budget-friendly guesthouses. The guide includes recommendations for different types of stays, ensuring that whether you're looking for a five-star retreat or a cozy homestay, you'll find the perfect place to rest. It also offers tips on how to book accommodations in advance or find last-minute deals.

Transportation options

Transportation in Vietnam can be both exciting and challenging. This guide explains the various modes of transport, from domestic flights and trains to motorbike rentals and buses. It provides advice on how to navigate the busy streets safely and what to expect when traveling between cities. You'll also learn about transportation apps that make getting around easier.

Practical Information

Practical information is covered extensively to help travelers feel prepared for their journey. This includes currency exchange, tipping etiquette, language basics, and safety tips. The guide ensures you're aware of the local customs and laws, so you can travel with confidence and respect for the culture.

Culinary delight

Culinary delights are one of Vietnam's greatest attractions, and this guide delves into the world of Vietnamese cuisine. From street food stalls to fine dining experiences, it highlights must-try dishes and where to find them. You'll learn about the regional variations in food and discover hidden gems where locals eat, enhancing your culinary adventure.

History and culture

Culture and heritage play a significant role in Vietnam's identity, and this guide provides an insightful look into the country's history, traditions, and festivals. It offers background on key cultural landmarks, temples, and museums, giving you a deeper understanding of Vietnam's rich past and how it influences the present.

Outdoor activities and adventure

Outdoor activities and adventures abound in Vietnam, from trekking through terraced rice fields to exploring caves and kayaking in Ha Long Bay. The guide lists popular outdoor destinations and suggests activities for every type of traveler, whether you're seeking adrenaline-pumping excursions or peaceful nature escapes. Exploring the regions of Vietnam, from the northern mountains to the southern Mekong Delta, offers diverse experiences. This guide provides detailed information on each region, including must-see attractions, off-the-beaten-path locales, and how to make the most of your time in each area. It helps you plan itineraries that fit your travel style and interests.

Useful website and apps

Travel resources and helpful links are included to ensure that visitors have all the tools they need. The guide offers suggestions for useful websites, travel apps, and other digital resources that enhance your trip. From booking tours to accessing emergency services, you'll find everything you need in one convenient place.

CHAPTER 2
GETTING STARTED

2.1 Understanding Vietnam

Understanding Vietnam requires immersing yourself in a country of contrasts, where ancient traditions intertwine with rapid modernization.

Location and Culture

Located in Southeast Asia, Vietnam stretches along the eastern edge of the Indochina Peninsula, bordered by China to the north, Laos and Cambodia to the west, and the South China Sea to the east. Its geography is as diverse as its culture, from bustling urban centers to serene countryside, from rugged mountains to tranquil beaches. A country shaped by centuries of history, Vietnam offers a rich tapestry of experiences that any traveler should embrace. The people of Vietnam are known for their hospitality and resilience. Deeply influenced by Confucian values, family plays a central role in Vietnamese life, and there's a strong emphasis on respect for elders and social harmony. Visitors will notice the warmth and friendliness of locals, who often go out of their way to help strangers, even with the challenge of language barriers. Learning a few basic Vietnamese phrases can open doors and make interactions more meaningful. While Vietnamese is the official language, English is increasingly spoken, especially in larger cities and tourist areas, making communication easier for visitors.

Transportation and climate

Vietnam operates at a unique pace, particularly in its cities. Ho Chi Minh City (formerly Saigon) in the south is fast, dynamic, and alive with modern energy. The streets are filled with motorbikes, markets, and a constant flow of life, a symbol of Vietnam's forward-looking spirit. On the other hand, Hanoi, the capital in the north, blends tradition with modernity. The city's ancient temples, French colonial architecture, and narrow streets of the Old Quarter evoke a sense of nostalgia and history. Life here seems to slow down a little, particularly around the city's lakes and peaceful parks, offering a balance to the city's hectic traffic and vibrant nightlife. Travelers should understand that Vietnam's weather is as varied as its regions. In the north, the climate can shift between cool winters and hot, humid summers, while the south remains tropical year-round with distinct wet and dry seasons. Packing appropriately for the region and season is essential, especially for those planning to explore the lush countryside or embark on adventures in the mountains.

Religion

Religion in Vietnam is diverse, with influences from Buddhism, Confucianism, Taoism, and a growing number of Catholics due to the country's colonial past. Temples and pagodas are scattered throughout the country, many of which are active places of worship. It's important for visitors to show respect when visiting these spiritual sites, dressing modestly and observing local customs. Religion and spirituality are deeply woven into the fabric of daily life, and you'll often see offerings of incense, food, or flowers left at shrines and altars, even in the busiest of cities.

Cuisines

Food is a significant part of understanding Vietnam's way of life. The country's cuisine is fresh, vibrant, and full of flavor, reflecting the diversity of its regions. Street food is a cornerstone of Vietnamese culture, and you'll find vendors selling everything from steaming bowls of pho to crispy banh mi sandwiches on nearly every corner. Mealtimes are communal, and sharing food is an important social activity. For many travelers, Vietnam's culinary scene is one of the most memorable aspects of their visit.

Economy and trade

In terms of economy and trade, Vietnam has seen rapid development in recent decades, yet much of its traditional ways of life remain intact. Agriculture, particularly rice farming, still plays a crucial role in rural areas. The sight of vast green rice terraces in the north and the floating markets of the Mekong Delta in the south offer a glimpse into the country's agricultural roots. Despite modernization, these time-honored practices continue to define much of Vietnam's rural life.

History

Travelers should also understand that Vietnam's history has shaped the identity of its people. From the ancient dynasties that ruled its lands to the struggles of colonial occupation and the Vietnam War, the country has endured and thrived. Museums, war relics, and historical landmarks such as the Cu Chi Tunnels and the Hoa Lo Prison provide a poignant reminder of Vietnam's turbulent past. However, today's Vietnam is very much a forward-looking nation, eager to embrace progress while holding tightly to its cultural heritage.

A blend of old and new

While Vietnam is modernizing at a rapid pace, its rural areas still reflect a slower, more traditional way of life. In the countryside, travelers can witness farming communities working the land, water buffaloes plowing the fields, and local artisans practicing crafts passed down through generations. It's a reminder that despite the country's push toward the future, its connection to the land and its traditions remains strong. Vietnam is a country of balance—between past and present, rural and urban, tradition and progress. To understand Vietnam is to appreciate this delicate equilibrium, to see the pride in its people's heritage, and to witness their ambition for the future. As a visitor, embracing these contrasts will not only deepen your understanding of the country but also create lasting memories of a place that captivates with every turn.

2.2 Geography, Climate & Best Time to Visit

The Geography of Vietnam

Vietnam's geography is as captivating as its culture, offering a diverse landscape that stretches over 1,600 kilometers along the eastern edge of the Indochina Peninsula. From the towering mountains of the north, where terraced rice fields cascade down lush hillsides, to the sprawling deltas of the south, the country presents a rich variety of natural beauty. The central region is marked by sandy beaches and dramatic coastal cliffs, while the Mekong Delta is a maze of rivers, swamps, and islands. The country's long coastline hugs the South China Sea, giving rise to breathtaking bays, vibrant fishing villages, and turquoise waters. Whether you're seeking mountains, rivers, or the sea, Vietnam's geography offers a perfect backdrop for adventure and exploration.

Climate and Weather Patterns

The climate of Vietnam is as varied as its geography, with three distinct regions experiencing different weather patterns throughout the year. In the north, the winters can be cool and misty, especially in mountainous areas like Sapa, while summers are hot and humid. Central Vietnam has a tropical climate, with a wet season from September to December, often bringing heavy rains and occasional typhoons. The south remains warm and tropical year-round, with a dry season from November to April and a wet season from May to October. This variety means that visitors will experience Vietnam differently depending on where and when they travel, adding an element of surprise and diversity to their journey.

Best Time to Visit Vietnam

The best time to visit Vietnam depends on which region you plan to explore, as the weather can be dramatically different from north to south. For those visiting the northern region, including Hanoi and Ha Long Bay, the spring months from March to April and autumn from September to November offer the most pleasant weather, with mild temperatures and little rain. In the central region, travelers should aim for February to May, avoiding the rainy season later in the year. The southern part of Vietnam, including Ho Chi Minh City and the Mekong Delta, is ideal during the dry season from November to February, when temperatures are moderate, and the skies are clear. Choosing the right time to visit can enhance your experience, as Vietnam's climate plays a significant role in shaping the landscape and atmosphere.

Exploring Vietnam Through Its Seasons

Exploring Vietnam's regions through different seasons adds an extra layer of magic to your journey. In the north, spring brings blooming flowers, especially in rural areas, where peach blossoms color the hillsides. The central beaches sparkle under the summer sun, making destinations like Da Nang and Nha Trang perfect for seaside escapes. Autumn turns the rice terraces in Sapa a golden hue, a striking contrast to the misty mountains. In the south, the dry season offers sunny skies for cruises along the Mekong or visits to floating markets. Each season breathes new life into the country, making every visit unique.

Practical Travel Tips for Visitors

When planning your trip, it's important to be mindful of the climate and its impact on your activities. Packing accordingly for the weather will make your experience more enjoyable, whether it's lightweight clothing for the tropical heat or warmer layers for cool northern nights. Visitors should also be aware of Vietnam's rainy seasons, as heavy downpours can affect travel plans, particularly in the central and southern regions. However, even during the rainy season, the landscape is lush and green, offering a different but equally beautiful experience. Being prepared for these variations in weather allows you to fully immerse yourself in Vietnam's ever-changing scenery and make the most of your visit.

2.3 History and Culture

The Rich History of Vietnam

Vietnam's history is a tapestry woven with tales of resistance, resilience, and renewal. It stretches back over 4,000 years, beginning with the legendary Hong Bang dynasty, believed to have founded the first Vietnamese state. Over centuries, the country faced invasions from powerful neighbors, notably China, which left a profound influence on Vietnam's culture and governance. The Vietnamese people, however, continuously fought for their independence, resulting in a unique identity that blends outside influences with strong local traditions. The 20th century saw Vietnam embroiled in struggles for independence, first from French colonial rule and later in the Vietnam War, a conflict that left deep scars but also solidified its spirit of unity and determination.

Cultural Heritage and Traditions

Vietnam's culture is a rich blend of indigenous traditions and foreign influences, shaped by thousands of years of interaction with other Asian civilizations, particularly China and India. Confucianism, Buddhism, and Taoism are deeply embedded in Vietnamese culture, affecting everything from art and architecture to family structures and social values. Visitors will find ancient temples alongside French colonial buildings, reflecting the country's layered history. Festivals are an essential aspect of life, with Tet, the Lunar New Year, being the most significant celebration. These cultural expressions offer travelers an immersive experience, where the old and the new coexist harmoniously, giving Vietnam its unique charm.

The Role of Family and Community

Family plays a central role in Vietnamese society, with multigenerational households being common, especially in rural areas. Respect for elders and ancestors is deeply ingrained, with many homes having an altar dedicated to those who have passed. This emphasis on family extends to a broader sense of community, where social harmony and cooperation are highly valued. Visitors will often experience the warmth of this community spirit in everyday interactions, whether it's through shared meals or the hospitality extended by locals. Understanding this cultural foundation can provide deeper insight into the rhythms of life in Vietnam, where relationships are often prioritized over individual pursuits.

Religion and Spiritual Life

Vietnam's spiritual landscape is diverse, influenced by Buddhism, Taoism, Confucianism, and more recently, Catholicism, introduced during the French colonial period. The country's numerous pagodas, temples, and churches reflect this blend of beliefs, where religious practices are seamlessly woven into daily life. Ancestor worship remains central, with people frequently visiting temples to make offerings for their ancestors, seeking blessings and good fortune. For travelers, visiting these sacred sites offers a window into the spiritual world of Vietnam, where religion is not just a personal matter but a community affair, interwoven with the country's history and identity.

Art, Music, and Traditional Craftsmanship

Vietnam's artistic traditions are deeply rooted in its history and culture, with ancient art forms like water puppetry, lacquer painting, and silk weaving still thriving today. These crafts tell stories of the country's past, often linked to myths, legends, and historical events. Traditional Vietnamese music is equally rich, with distinct regional styles and instruments like the monochord zither or the bamboo flute. In cities like Hanoi or Hue, visitors can experience these artistic traditions firsthand, either in performance or by visiting workshops where craftsmen keep centuries-old skills alive. The art and music of Vietnam provide a sensory journey that deepens one's understanding of its culture.

Modern-Day Vietnam and Cultural Evolution

While Vietnam has rapidly modernized in recent decades, it remains deeply connected to its past, with a cultural evolution that balances tradition and progress. Urban centers like Ho Chi Minh City and Hanoi are filled with modern skyscrapers, international businesses, and bustling nightlife, yet ancient traditions still linger in the fabric of daily life. Farmers still work the fields as their ancestors did, while city dwellers embrace technology and global trends. This balance between old and new is one of Vietnam's defining characteristics, making it a fascinating destination for travelers looking to experience both its historical roots and its contemporary vibrancy.

2.4 Cultural Do's and Don'ts

Respect for Elders and Hierarchy

In Vietnam, respect for elders is a deeply ingrained part of the culture. This respect extends to all forms of social interaction, from how one addresses someone older to offering the first greeting or gift to the most senior person in a group. When visiting Vietnamese homes or engaging with locals, it's important to acknowledge the hierarchy, whether in families or in formal settings. A simple gesture like a respectful bow or offering both hands when presenting a gift can convey your understanding of their customs. Visitors should always remain mindful of these subtleties, as they reflect the deeply rooted values of harmony and respect in society.

Dress Modestly in Temples and Sacred Places

Vietnam is home to numerous temples, pagodas, and sacred sites, where visitors are welcome but must adhere to cultural norms regarding behavior and attire. Dressing modestly is essential when visiting these places, as revealing clothing is considered disrespectful. Shoulders should be covered, and wearing long pants or skirts is advisable. Before entering a temple, it's customary to remove your shoes, and silence is often expected to maintain the sanctity of the space. Following these unwritten rules not only shows respect for the local culture but also allows visitors to experience the spiritual tranquility these places offer.

Table Manners and Eating Etiquette

Dining in Vietnam is a communal affair, with meals often shared in groups and served family-style. When eating, it's customary to wait for the eldest person to begin before taking your first bite. Chopsticks are the primary utensils, and knowing how to handle them properly is important, especially since certain actions, like sticking chopsticks upright in a bowl of rice, are considered bad luck as they resemble incense sticks used in funerals. Visitors should also be mindful of not leaving too much food on their plate, as it can be seen as wasteful. By observing these dining customs, travelers can show respect for the shared values of hospitality and togetherness in Vietnam.

Greetings and Social Interactions

The Vietnamese greet each other with a gentle handshake or a slight bow, though the latter is more common in formal or elder interactions. For visitors, learning to say basic phrases like "xin chào" (hello) or "cảm ơn" (thank you) can go a long way in building rapport with locals. Public displays of affection, such as hugging or kissing, are not common and are generally frowned upon, especially in rural areas. Instead, politeness and restraint are valued in social interactions. Understanding and adhering to these norms can make your stay in Vietnam more pleasant and foster positive connections with the people you meet.

Handling Money and Gifts

Exchanging money or giving gifts is often done with both hands, which is seen as a sign of respect. When making purchases or paying for services, handing money with both hands shows your acknowledgment of this cultural value. Similarly, when giving gifts, it's customary to offer them with both hands, and wrapping the gift in colorful paper, especially in red or gold, is considered auspicious. On the other hand, black and white are associated with mourning and should be avoided for gift wrapping. Understanding these cultural nuances around gifting and transactions helps visitors navigate social exchanges with grace and respect.

Mindful Communication and Body Language

Vietnamese communication tends to be indirect, especially when it comes to sensitive topics. People often avoid confrontational language, preferring to maintain harmony in conversations. Raising your voice, expressing frustration, or using aggressive gestures can be considered rude and disrespectful. Visitors should be aware of their tone and body language, using calm and polite communication, especially in public settings. Smiling and maintaining a friendly demeanor goes a long way in Vietnam, where non-verbal cues are just as important as the spoken word. Being mindful of this aspect of Vietnamese culture helps foster positive interactions and ensures you are seen as a respectful visitor.

Respect for Local Customs and Beliefs

Throughout Vietnam, traditions and customs are observed in both rural and urban areas, reflecting the country's rich cultural tapestry. Many Vietnamese people still practice ancestor worship, and visitors may see small altars in homes or businesses. It's important to show respect around these sacred spaces, refraining from touching or disturbing offerings. Additionally, photography in certain religious or sacred areas may be restricted, so it's always polite to ask for permission before taking photos. Understanding and respecting these local beliefs and practices allows visitors to engage more meaningfully with the culture, ensuring a harmonious and enriching experience.

2.5 Language, Communication & Essential Vietnamese Phrases

The language landscape of Vietnam is as rich and diverse as its culture. Vietnamese is the official language, and it is spoken by the majority of the population. Its unique tonal nature can make it seem complex to outsiders, with six distinct tones that change the meaning of words. This linguistic system reflects the country's long history and its influences, particularly from China, as Vietnamese uses a modified Latin script introduced by French missionaries. While English is becoming more widespread, especially in urban centers, learning some basic Vietnamese phrases can greatly enhance a visitor's experience, helping them navigate the culture more seamlessly.

Understanding Vietnamese Language and Pronunciation

Vietnamese, unlike many other Asian languages, uses a Romanized alphabet, which makes it more accessible for Western travelers. However, it is a tonal language, meaning the pitch or tone of a word can change its meaning entirely. There are six tones in northern dialects, and they are crucial to communication. Mispronouncing a tone can lead to confusion, as the same word spoken with a different tone could mean something completely different. While this may seem daunting at first, even mastering a few simple words with correct pronunciation can open doors to deeper cultural exchanges and show a visitor's respect for the local language.

Communicating with Locals

Communication in Vietnam is generally warm and polite, but it is also indirect, especially when addressing sensitive topics. Locals tend to avoid direct refusals or confrontations, often opting for non-verbal cues or subtle expressions of disagreement. When interacting with Vietnamese people, a soft tone and courteous demeanor go a long way. Visitors should be aware that body language is an important aspect of communication here. A smile is often used to ease awkwardness or to express understanding. In more rural areas, English may not be widely spoken, so using basic Vietnamese phrases or even gestures can help bridge the communication gap and foster positive interactions.

Useful Vietnamese Phrases for Travelers

Learning a few basic Vietnamese phrases can not only help with everyday situations like ordering food or asking for directions but also shows a level of respect and interest in the local culture. Simple greetings such as "xin chào" (hello) or "cảm ơn" (thank you) are greatly appreciated by locals. The effort to speak Vietnamese, even if imperfect, often results in warm smiles and enthusiastic responses from the people. For travelers, mastering phrases like "bao nhiêu?" (how much?) and "xin lỗi" (excuse me) can prove incredibly useful in markets or crowded places. These small exchanges provide a glimpse into the friendly nature of Vietnamese people and create a more immersive travel experience.

Navigating Language Barriers

Although Vietnamese is the dominant language, many younger Vietnamese, especially in major cities like Hanoi and Ho Chi Minh City, speak some English, thanks to its inclusion in school curriculums and the rise of tourism. In tourist-heavy areas, you may find signage, menus, and even tour guides available in English. However, in rural or less touristy areas, the language barrier can be more prominent. Carrying a translation app or a small phrasebook can be helpful when traveling off the beaten path. Patience and a willingness to engage with locals, even through gestures or body language, can turn these interactions into memorable and rewarding experiences.

The Importance of Cultural Sensitivity in Communication

Respecting the cultural nuances of communication is vital when visiting Vietnam. Visitors should be aware of the indirect nature of Vietnamese communication, especially when dealing with older generations or formal situations. When speaking to elders or figures of authority, using a softer tone and maintaining respectful body language can convey the appropriate respect. It is also important to avoid being too assertive or loud, as this may come off as disrespectful. Politeness is key, and even when communication barriers arise, remaining calm and patient will be appreciated. Understanding these unspoken rules of communication helps visitors engage more meaningfully with the local culture.

Building Connections through Language

Learning even a few words of Vietnamese can transform a visitor's experience from simply touring the country to truly connecting with its people. Locals often admire travelers who make an effort to speak their language, even if the pronunciation isn't perfect. These attempts to communicate in the native tongue foster goodwill and often lead to deeper connections. Whether bargaining in a market, ordering a traditional dish, or simply greeting someone on the street, using Vietnamese shows a traveler's willingness to step outside their comfort zone and embrace the local way of life. This engagement enriches not only the travel experience but also the connections made along the way.

The Future of Language in Vietnam

As Vietnam continues to grow economically and culturally on the global stage, English is becoming more prominent, particularly in business and education. However, Vietnamese remains at the heart of the country's identity, shaping everything from everyday interactions to national pride. For visitors, understanding this balance between the global and the local is essential in navigating the linguistic landscape of Vietnam. While English may offer convenience in cities, Vietnamese opens doors to authentic cultural exchanges. Embracing both languages during a visit to Vietnam allows for a richer, more meaningful travel experience, bridging the gap between tourist and local in an increasingly connected world.

2.6 Currency and Money Matters

Navigating currency exchange and banking services is an important aspect of any travel experience in Vietnam. As a foreign visitor, understanding the local currency, exchange rates, and the accessibility of banking services is crucial for a smooth stay. Vietnam uses the Vietnamese dong (VND), a currency that reflects the unique rhythm of the country's economy. While major cities offer an array of exchange options and banking conveniences, visitors should be prepared for a different experience in rural areas. Ensuring you have the right knowledge about currency exchange and banking practices will help you avoid unnecessary hassles and make your trip more enjoyable.

Understanding the Vietnamese Dong

The official currency of Vietnam is the Vietnamese dong (VND), which is used in all transactions, from paying for street food to purchasing souvenirs. The dong is often noted for its high denominations, with notes ranging from 1,000 VND to 500,000 VND, which can initially be overwhelming for visitors unfamiliar with handling such large numbers. The exchange rate for foreign currencies, particularly the US dollar or euro, fluctuates but remains relatively favorable for travelers, making Vietnam a budget-friendly destination. Carrying small denominations of dong is essential, especially when traveling outside the major cities where cash is preferred over card payments.

Currency Exchange Options for Travelers

Currency exchange in Vietnam is straightforward in the more urban areas, with options ranging from banks, hotels, and authorized exchange bureaus. Banks generally offer the most reliable exchange rates, though there may be small fees involved. Visitors arriving at major airports like Noi Bai or Tan Son Nhat will find numerous exchange counters that offer competitive rates. In tourist-heavy areas such as Hanoi and Ho Chi Minh City, exchanging money is easy, and ATMs are widely available. However, in rural regions or smaller towns, it can be more challenging, so it's advisable to exchange money beforehand or carry sufficient dong for daily needs.

Banking Services and ATM Accessibility

Vietnam's banking system is modernizing rapidly, and visitors can access a wide range of banking services during their stay. Most major cities have an abundance of ATMs that accept foreign credit and debit cards, allowing for convenient cash withdrawals in VND. International banks such as HSBC, ANZ, and Citi have branches in Vietnam, providing services familiar to international travelers. However, ATM withdrawal fees may vary depending on the bank, and some ATMs impose limits on how much cash can be withdrawn per transaction. Visitors should ensure their home bank cards are enabled for international use and notify their bank of travel plans to avoid potential issues.

Credit Cards and Payment Methods

While Vietnam is becoming more accommodating of cashless transactions, cash remains the dominant form of payment, particularly in local markets, small restaurants, and rural areas. Major hotels, restaurants, and shopping malls in cities like Ho Chi Minh City and Hanoi accept international credit cards such as Visa and MasterCard, but outside these areas, reliance on cash is often necessary. Travelers should also be aware of transaction fees that may be incurred when using credit cards, as well as the occasional preference for cash even in places that technically accept cards. Carrying a mix of cash and cards is the most practical approach for a smooth experience.

Safety and Security in Currency Exchange

As with any international destination, safety and security should be top priorities when handling money in Vietnam. Authorized currency exchange points such as banks and exchange bureaus offer safe and reliable services, while black market exchanges, though tempting with their seemingly better rates, should be avoided due to the risks of counterfeit currency and fraud. It's always advisable to count your money carefully after any exchange and keep receipts in case of any discrepancies. When using ATMs, choose machines located in well-lit, secure areas such as inside bank branches or major hotels to minimize the risk of theft or card skimming.

Banking Hours and Services for Tourists

Vietnamese banks generally operate from Monday to Friday, opening at around 8 AM and closing between 4 and 5 PM, with some banks offering limited hours on Saturday mornings. However, ATMs are accessible 24 hours a day in urban areas, providing flexibility for visitors needing to withdraw cash at any time. For those looking to perform more complex banking tasks, such as wiring money or opening temporary accounts, it is recommended to visit during regular banking hours and to bring identification, such as a passport, to complete transactions. Travelers should familiarize themselves with the local banking hours to avoid any inconveniences.

Foreign Currency Acceptance in Vietnam

Although the official currency is the dong, US dollars are sometimes accepted in tourist areas and high-end establishments, particularly in Ho Chi Minh City and Hanoi. However, this practice is becoming less common, and visitors should not rely on the ability to pay with foreign currencies. If using dollars, it's important to carry bills in pristine condition, as torn or worn-out notes are often rejected. Nevertheless, for a smoother and more authentic experience, it is recommended to use Vietnamese dong for all transactions, which also allows for better budgeting and understanding of local prices. For visitors, it is essential to manage currency wisely when traveling in Vietnam. While it is easy to exchange money in major cities, rural areas may not offer the same convenience, making it prudent to plan ahead. Avoid carrying large sums of money in public, and use a money belt or secure pouch for cash and cards. It's also advisable to keep some smaller denominations handy for tips or small purchases, as vendors often have difficulty providing change for large bills. Being mindful of currency management can greatly enhance the ease and enjoyment of traveling in Vietnam.

CHAPTER 3
PLANNING YOUR TRIP

3.1 Visa and Entry Requirements

When planning a trip to Vietnam, understanding the visa requirements and entry procedures is crucial for a smooth and enjoyable experience. Vietnam offers several options for visas depending on your nationality, length of stay, and the purpose of your visit. For many travelers, a visa is required before entering the country, although some nationalities are granted short visa exemptions for tourism purposes. Vietnam has simplified the visa application process in recent years, with options like electronic visas (e-visa) and visas on arrival, allowing for more flexibility and convenience when planning your journey.

Applying for a Visa to Vietnam

For travelers who need a visa, the most common method is to apply for an e-visa online. This option is available for citizens of over 80 countries and is valid for a stay of up to 30 days. The process involves filling out an online application form, submitting a passport-sized photo, and paying a processing fee. Once approved, the e-visa allows entry through designated international airports and land border crossings. This process eliminates the need to visit an embassy or consulate, making it a popular choice for tourists. For longer stays or multiple-entry visas, applying at a Vietnamese embassy remains an option.

Visa on Arrival for Travelers

Another convenient option for visitors is the Visa on Arrival (VOA) program, which allows travelers to obtain their visa upon arrival at one of Vietnam's international airports. However, it's important to note that this option requires travelers to apply for an approval letter from a recognized travel agency before departing for Vietnam. Once the approval letter is received, visitors present it at the visa counter upon arrival, where they pay a stamping fee and receive their visa. This method is especially useful for those planning a last-minute trip or for visitors who need a longer visa duration than an e-visa allows.

Visa Exemptions and Special Cases

Vietnam offers visa exemptions to citizens of several countries, typically for short visits of 15 to 30 days. This exemption allows travelers to enter the country without a visa, provided their stay is within the allowed time frame. For visitors from countries like Japan, South Korea, and members of the ASEAN region, these exemptions are particularly beneficial for brief holidays or

25

business trips. However, if you plan to stay longer or enter Vietnam multiple times, you will need to apply for the appropriate visa. Travelers should check the latest regulations, as visa exemption rules can vary depending on diplomatic agreements and regional policies.

Entry Procedures at Vietnam's Borders

Once your visa is in order, entering Vietnam is a straightforward process. Upon arrival at any international airport, land border crossing, or seaport, travelers must present their passport, visa, or e-visa approval, and any necessary supporting documents. Immigration officials will process your documents and grant you entry. For those using the Visa on Arrival service, ensure you have the approval letter, passport-sized photos, and sufficient funds to cover the stamping fee. The entry process typically runs smoothly, but it's advisable to have copies of all relevant documents in case of any issues.

Health and Safety Requirements for Entry

In addition to the visa and immigration formalities, travelers should also be aware of any health and safety entry requirements. Vietnam may require proof of vaccinations, especially for travelers arriving from regions with specific health risks. During global health events such as pandemics, additional entry measures such as health declarations, quarantine regulations, or proof of a negative COVID-19 test may be implemented. It's essential to check the latest health advisories from the Vietnamese government or your embassy before traveling. Being prepared with all necessary health documentation ensures a seamless entry process and contributes to the overall safety of your visit.

Extending Your Stay in Vietnam

If you wish to extend your stay beyond the duration of your visa, Vietnam offers several options to extend or renew your visa while you are still in the country. Visitors can apply for a visa extension through travel agencies or at local immigration offices. The extension process typically requires submitting an application form, your passport, and the current visa, along with the appropriate fees. The length of the extension depends on your visa type, but most travelers can extend their stay by 30 days. Planning ahead and allowing time for the processing of visa extensions is crucial to avoid any overstays or legal issues.

Departure Procedures and Re-Entry

When your trip to Vietnam comes to an end, the departure procedures are relatively simple. Travelers need to present their passport and visa at immigration control when leaving the country. For those who have overstayed their visa, fines may apply, and resolving this before departure is necessary to avoid further complications. If you plan to return to Vietnam during the same trip, a multiple-entry visa is recommended to facilitate re-entry without needing to apply for a new visa each time. Ensuring all visa details are in order before departing will help avoid unnecessary delays or issues at the airport.

3.2 Packing Essentials

Clothing and footwear

When planning a trip to Vietnam, ensuring you have the right items packed is key to enjoying a smooth and memorable journey. Given the diverse climate across the country, travelers should consider packing light, breathable clothing suitable for Vietnam's tropical heat, as well as warmer layers for cooler regions or mountainous areas. Light, comfortable shoes are essential for exploring both the urban landscapes and rural areas, where you may encounter uneven terrain or need to walk long distances. Having appropriate footwear ensures you can experience Vietnam's stunning landscapes without discomfort.

Health and Safety essential

Bringing along a travel-sized first aid kit is also highly recommended, containing basic items like bandages, antiseptic, and any prescription medication you might need. Vietnam's street food culture is vibrant, but those unfamiliar with local ingredients might want to pack anti-diarrheal medication or treatments for upset stomachs. Sun protection is another must-have, especially for travelers venturing to beach destinations or spending extended periods outdoors. Sunglasses, sunscreen, and a wide-brimmed hat can shield you from the intense tropical sun, keeping you comfortable during outdoor adventures.

Electronics

In terms of technology, packing a portable power bank and adapters for Vietnam's outlets will ensure you stay connected, especially when exploring remote areas. Vietnam uses the 220V electrical system, and depending on where you're coming from, you might need an adapter to charge your devices. It's also smart to carry a lightweight daypack for your daily excursions, as it allows you to store essential items like water, a camera, and any souvenirs you might pick

27

up during the day. Being able to carry your belongings comfortably makes sightseeing far more enjoyable.

Documentation

For practical travel documentation, it's important to have printed copies of your passport, visa, and any other essential documents. While digital copies are convenient, having hard copies ensures you're prepared in case of emergencies or loss of access to your phone. Having a small money belt or secure pouch to store these items, along with some local currency, will help you keep important belongings safe from pickpockets, particularly in crowded markets or urban areas. Vietnam's currency is the Vietnamese dong, and carrying smaller bills is useful for markets and rural areas where card payment may not be available.

Personal items

A good insect repellent is vital, especially if you plan to explore Vietnam's more rural or jungle areas where mosquitoes are common. Applying repellent can help prevent bites and reduce the risk of mosquito-borne illnesses. Additionally, a rain jacket or compact umbrella is a smart choice during the rainy season, allowing you to stay dry without taking up too much space in your luggage. By carefully considering these packing essentials, you'll be well-prepared to embrace all that Vietnam has to offer, from its bustling cities to its serene landscapes.

3.3 Budgeting for Your Trip

Vietnam is a destination known for its affordability, making it a popular choice for travelers seeking an enriching experience without breaking the bank. However, to fully enjoy what the country has to offer, it's essential to plan your travel budget carefully. Start by considering your main expenses, such as accommodation, food, transportation, and activities. Vietnam offers a wide range of options for all budgets, from luxury hotels and gourmet dining to budget hostels and street food, giving you the flexibility to tailor your trip based on your spending preferences.

Accommodation and transportation cost

When it comes to accommodation, the cost can vary significantly depending on where you choose to stay and the level of comfort you prefer. Major cities like Ho Chi Minh City and Hanoi tend to have pricier options, while smaller towns and rural areas offer more budget-friendly alternatives. Transportation within

Vietnam is another aspect to consider in your budget. Domestic flights are affordable, but buses and trains are even cheaper, allowing you to explore the country's diverse regions. Ensure you factor in transport costs between cities and for daily excursions.

Dining and food expenses

Food in Vietnam is both delicious and budget-friendly, with street food providing an authentic and inexpensive way to experience the country's culinary delights. Dining in local restaurants is affordable, but high-end restaurants in urban centers can add to your overall costs. For activities, Vietnam offers a range of affordable or even free experiences, such as visiting temples, hiking in the mountains, or exploring rural villages. However, guided tours, entrance fees to major attractions, and activities like boat trips in Ha Long Bay or Mekong Delta tours will add to your budget, so it's important to plan for those in advance.

Currency exchange rates

Currency exchange rates can also impact your travel budget, so keeping an eye on the Vietnamese dong (VND) to your home currency will help you make more accurate financial preparations. It's a good idea to carry both cash and a credit card for flexibility, but be aware that some rural areas may not accept card payments. For a smooth experience, set aside an emergency fund for unforeseen expenses like medical needs, transportation changes, or additional activities that may come up during your travels.

3.4 Accommodation Options

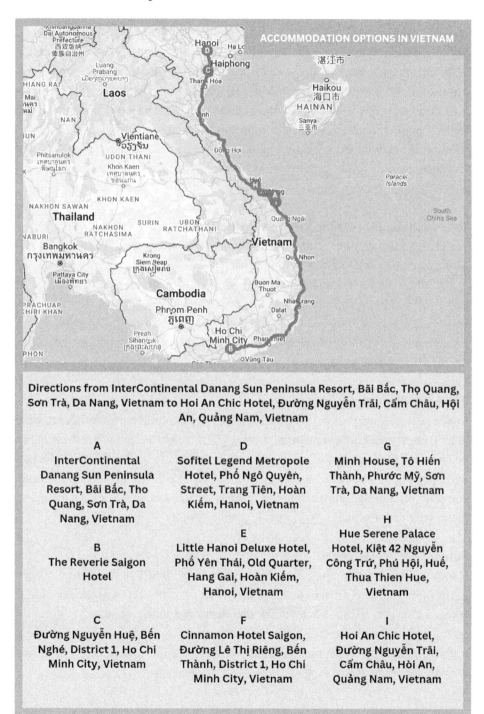

Directions from InterContinental Danang Sun Peninsula Resort, Bãi Bắc, Thọ Quang, Sơn Trà, Da Nang, Vietnam to Hoi An Chic Hotel, Đường Nguyễn Trãi, Cẩm Châu, Hội An, Quảng Nam, Vietnam

A
InterContinental Danang Sun Peninsula Resort, Bãi Bắc, Tho Quang, Sơn Trà, Da Nang, Vietnam

B
The Reverie Saigon Hotel

C
Đường Nguyễn Huệ, Bến Nghé, District 1, Ho Chi Minh City, Vietnam

D
Sofitel Legend Metropole Hotel, Phố Ngô Quyền, Street, Trang Tiên, Hoàn Kiếm, Hanoi, Vietnam

E
Little Hanoi Deluxe Hotel, Phố Yên Thái, Old Quarter, Hang Gai, Hoàn Kiếm, Hanoi, Vietnam

F
Cinnamon Hotel Saigon, Đường Lê Thị Riêng, Bến Thành, District 1, Ho Chi Minh City, Vietnam

G
Minh House, Tô Hiến Thành, Phước Mỹ, Sơn Trà, Da Nang, Vietnam

H
Hue Serene Palace Hotel, Kiệt 42 Nguyễn Công Trứ, Phú Hội, Huế, Thua Thien Hue, Vietnam

I
Hoi An Chic Hotel, Đường Nguyễn Trãi, Cẩm Châu, Hòi An, Quảng Nam, Vietnam

Luxury Hotels in Vietnam

Reverie saigon hotel

For those seeking the utmost in luxury, The Reverie Saigon in Ho Chi Minh City is an exceptional choice. Located in the heart of District 1, this stunning hotel offers rooms starting at approximately $350 per night. With its lavish European-style décor and world-class service, guests can enjoy amenities like a rooftop pool, spa, and several fine dining restaurants. The opulent interiors and panoramic views of the city make it a perfect haven for relaxation and indulgence. For more information or reservations, visit their website at www.thereveriesaigon.com.

InterContinental Danang Sun Peninsula Resort

Another luxury option is the InterContinental Danang Sun Peninsula Resort, located in Da Nang. Nestled within a private bay on the Son Tra Peninsula, this resort offers rooms from $400 per night. Known for its breathtaking ocean views and eco-friendly design, the hotel boasts private villas, an award-winning spa, and exclusive beach access. Guests can also enjoy the fine dining experience at La Maison 1888, one of Vietnam's top restaurants. For booking and further details, the official website is www.danang.intercontinental.com.

Emeralda Resort

In the picturesque region of Ninh Binh, the Emeralda Resort Ninh Binh offers luxury in a peaceful countryside setting. The resort is surrounded by natural beauty and features traditional Vietnamese architecture. Prices start at around $150 per night. The resort includes a full-service spa, two swimming pools, and eco-tours that allow guests to explore the stunning landscapes of Ninh Binh. To make reservations, visit www.emeraldaresort.com.

Sofitel Legend Metropole

Hanoi's luxury accommodation options are exemplified by Sofitel Legend Metropole Hanoi. This iconic hotel offers an elegant stay with prices starting from $250 per night. Located in the historic French Quarter, it combines colonial charm with modern luxury. Guests can enjoy the hotel's spa, fine dining options, and explore the city's attractions within walking distance. The official website for reservations is www.sofitel-legend-metropole-hanoi.com.

Six Senses Ninh Van Bay

Six Senses Ninh Van Bay in Nha Trang offers an unparalleled luxurious experience with villas starting at $500 per night. Located on a secluded peninsula, accessible only by boat, this resort offers guests privacy, stunning views, and an emphasis on wellness. The resort's spa and eco-friendly design provide a perfect escape into nature. Visit their website for more information at www.sixsenses.com/ninhvanbay.

Budget friendly options
Cinnamon Hotel Saigon

Cinnamon Hotel Saigon in Ho Chi Minh City is a budget-friendly option with rooms starting at $40 per night. Located close to the city's major attractions, this hotel offers a cozy, modern experience with comfortable rooms and personalized service. Visitors can easily explore nearby markets and cultural landmarks. For reservations, visit https://cinnamon-hotel-saigon-ho-chi-minh-city.hotel-dir.com/en/.

Little Hanoi Deluxe Hotel

Another excellent budget choice is Little Hanoi Deluxe Hotel in Hanoi, offering rooms from $30 per night. The hotel is centrally located in the Old Quarter, making it convenient for exploring Hanoi's historic sites. Despite its affordable price, it provides clean, comfortable rooms and a complimentary breakfast. For bookings, visit http://www.littlehanoideluxehotel.com/.

Minh house

In Da Nang, the Minh House offers an affordable yet charming stay with rooms priced from $35 per night. This boutique hotel combines modern design with traditional Vietnamese touches, offering guests a quiet retreat near the city center. Guests can enjoy a small pool, breakfast, and easy access to the beach. For more information, visit https://minh-house.danang-hotels.com/en/.

Hue Serene Palace Hotel

The Hue Serene Palace Hotel in Hue provides budget-conscious travelers with an excellent option at around $25 per night. Located close to the Imperial City, this hotel is ideal for those interested in Hue's rich history. It offers clean rooms, friendly service, and convenient access to the city's main attractions. The hotel's website is https://www.serenepalacehotel.com/.

Hoi An chic hotel

In the peaceful town of Hoi An, Hoi An Chic Hotel provides an affordable option starting at $50 per night. This boutique hotel is surrounded by rice paddies and offers a tranquil atmosphere. Guests can enjoy bicycle rentals, a pool, and complimentary breakfast. For bookings, visit www.hoianchic.com.

3.5 Transportation Options

Navigating Vietnam's cities and towns through public transportation is an experience that allows visitors to immerse themselves in the local way of life. The country offers a wide array of transportation options, ranging from buses and trains to motorbike taxis, each providing a unique way to explore the urban and rural landscapes. Understanding how to navigate these options will ensure a smooth journey for visitors, as they travel through bustling cities or along the scenic coastlines.

Bus system

The most common form of public transportation in major cities like Hanoi and Ho Chi Minh City is the bus system. Buses are affordable and extensive, covering a vast network of routes that connect different districts. Bus fares typically range from 7,000 to 10,000 VND (about 30 to 50 cents USD), making them a cost-effective choice for budget travelers. Most buses are equipped with air conditioning, and routes are marked in both Vietnamese and English, which helps foreign visitors navigate more easily. Visitors can either pay the fare directly to the driver or purchase a monthly pass for longer stays. Apps like BusMap can also be downloaded to track routes and schedules, making navigation easier.

Motorbike and Taxis

Motorbike taxis, known as "xe ôm," are a popular and convenient way to get around in Vietnam, particularly for shorter distances or areas that are not accessible by buses. Motorbike taxis can be hailed from almost any corner of a city, and the fare is usually negotiated before the ride, though apps like Grab and Gojek have standardized the pricing. Prices typically start from 10,000 VND for short trips, with rates increasing based on distance. Using motorbike taxis is not only fast but also offers a more immersive experience as you zip through traffic, experiencing the city up close. It's important for visitors to ensure that their driver provides a helmet, as wearing one is required by law.

Train system

For those traveling longer distances between cities or exploring the countryside, Vietnam's train network provides a scenic and comfortable option. The Reunification Express, which runs from Hanoi to Ho Chi Minh City, is one of the most famous train routes in Southeast Asia. The journey can take up to 35 hours, but many travelers opt to break up the trip with stops in destinations like Hue or Da Nang. Prices for train tickets vary depending on the class, with seats starting around 500,000 VND (approximately 20 USD) and sleeper cabins costing more. Visitors are encouraged to book tickets in advance, especially during holiday seasons, through official websites or travel agencies.

Metro system

In addition to buses, motorbike taxis, and trains, Vietnam's cities are gradually adopting metro systems. Ho Chi Minh City, for instance, is currently developing its first metro line, which will offer an efficient way to travel across the sprawling urban area. Though the metro system is still in its early stages, once completed, it will provide an additional option for avoiding the city's notorious traffic congestion. Ticket prices are expected to be affordable, similar to bus fares, making it accessible to both locals and tourists.

Renting of vehicles

For visitors who prefer to explore at their own pace, renting a bicycle or motorbike is a popular option, especially in cities like Hoi An, Da Nang, and smaller towns. Bicycle rentals can cost as little as 40,000 VND per day (approximately 1.50 USD), while motorbike rentals range from 100,000 to 150,000 VND per day (about 4 to 6 USD). Renting a motorbike offers flexibility, allowing visitors to venture off the beaten path to discover Vietnam's hidden gems. However, it's crucial for travelers to be aware of the local traffic rules and ensure they have the proper license if driving a motorbike. For longer journeys or more convenient city transfers, taxis are widely available and relatively affordable in Vietnam. Reputable taxi companies, such as Mai Linh and Vinasun, operate in most cities and are known for using meters to calculate fares. A short ride within the city will generally cost around 50,000 to 100,000 VND (2 to 4 USD), depending on the distance. Visitors should be cautious when taking unmetered taxis and are advised to use ride-hailing apps like Grab, which ensure transparency in pricing and provide the convenience of cashless payments.

34

Practical information

Additionally, Vietnam's coastal cities and islands are accessible through a network of ferries and boats. Popular routes include the ferry from Ho Chi Minh City to Vung Tau or from the mainland to Phu Quoc Island. These ferries are a scenic way to travel and offer a relaxing journey across Vietnam's picturesque waterways. Prices vary depending on the destination, with fares typically starting around 100,000 VND (approximately 4 USD). It's recommended to check schedules in advance and arrive early to ensure a spot on the ferry, especially during peak travel seasons. To further ease navigation, visitors are encouraged to download apps such as Grab or Gojek, which not only provide taxi and motorbike services but also offer carpooling and delivery options. These apps allow travelers to input their destinations in English, making it easier for those who are not fluent in Vietnamese to get around. With GPS and real-time tracking, the apps help ensure that visitors are always on the right route, eliminating the potential for misunderstandings or overcharging.

CHAPTER 4
EXPLORING HANOI

4.1 Overview of Hanoi

Hanoi, the capital of Vietnam, is a city that vibrates with energy, history, and cultural richness. Nestled in the northern part of the country, it seamlessly blends its past with modernity, offering visitors a unique experience that captures the essence of Vietnam's soul. For those arriving in Hanoi, the city unfolds like a fascinating story where centuries-old temples, tree-lined boulevards, and colonial architecture intermingle with a bustling urban landscape. The Old Quarter, with its labyrinth of narrow streets, embodies the city's ancient heart, while the French Quarter echoes with remnants of its colonial past. Every corner of Hanoi tells a different tale, giving visitors the chance to explore both its heritage and the contemporary vibrancy that defines modern Vietnam.

Historic and cultural significance

Walking through Hanoi, one can feel the weight of history as well as the excitement of a city constantly evolving. Its many historical landmarks, like the Ho Chi Minh Mausoleum and the Temple of Literature, offer visitors a glimpse into Vietnam's profound history, deeply intertwined with its resilient identity. Each site is more than just a tourist attraction; it serves as a bridge between the past and present. Whether visiting the serene Hoan Kiem Lake, where locals practice tai chi at sunrise, or wandering through the sprawling markets full of colorful fabrics, spices, and local delicacies, visitors find themselves immersed in an atmosphere that is authentically Vietnamese. One of the things that make Hanoi a standout destination is the way its culture is reflected in everyday life. From the ubiquitous food stalls serving fragrant bowls of pho to the traditional water puppet shows that have entertained generations, the city embraces its traditions with pride. Visitors will quickly notice the importance of food in daily life here, with street vendors and bustling markets offering an array of dishes that capture the flavors of northern Vietnam. The street food culture in Hanoi is famous, and indulging in dishes like bun cha or banh mi from a roadside stall is as much a cultural experience as it is a culinary delight. These vibrant food scenes offer a direct connection to the city's heart, where every dish is steeped in history and local pride. While the historical aspects of Hanoi are fascinating, the city is also known for its modern side. Sleek skyscrapers rise alongside the old colonial buildings, and the city is rapidly developing into a contemporary metropolis. Modern cafes, trendy boutiques, and upscale restaurants are popping up across the city, catering to a younger generation and tourists looking for a cosmopolitan experience. Yet, despite the rapid modernization, Hanoi retains its soul, ensuring that progress doesn't erase its distinct charm. The balance between old and new gives Hanoi a multifaceted personality, making it a city that offers something for every kind of traveler.

Transportation

Navigating Hanoi is relatively easy, with various transportation options available to visitors. Motorbikes dominate the roads, creating a constant hum of activity, and they are also a popular way for tourists to explore the city. For those less inclined to hop on the back of a motorbike, the city's expanding public transportation network offers affordable and efficient alternatives. Buses, taxis, and the newly developing metro system are all convenient for getting around Hanoi's many districts. Walking, however, remains one of the best ways to explore the city, particularly around the Old Quarter, where the chaotic charm of Hanoi comes alive in the small, busy streets.

Best time to visit

The best time to visit Hanoi is in the spring (March to April) or autumn (September to November) when the weather is cool and comfortable. During these months, the city bursts with colors, and the streets are alive with festivals and events. Hanoi's winters are relatively mild, though it can get quite chilly, especially compared to the southern regions of Vietnam. Summer brings heat and humidity, as well as the monsoon rains, which can sometimes disrupt travel plans. Nevertheless, Hanoi remains a year-round destination for those eager to discover its hidden gems, rich history, and cultural vibrancy.

Shopping and souvenirs

Shopping in Hanoi is another delightful experience. The markets and boutiques offer a variety of goods, from traditional silk garments to handcrafted pottery and art. The vibrant Dong Xuan Market is particularly famous for its wide range of local products and is the perfect place for visitors to pick up unique souvenirs. Bargaining is expected, and for many, it's an enjoyable part of the shopping experience, giving travelers an opportunity to interact more closely with locals. For those seeking high-end items, the French Quarter offers upscale shops with a mix of international and local brands, providing a different flavor of Hanoi's retail culture.

Outdoor adventures

Hanoi is also a gateway to explore the breathtaking natural beauty surrounding it. A short trip outside the city leads to Ha Long Bay, a UNESCO World Heritage Site famed for its emerald waters and towering limestone islands. The lush countryside surrounding Hanoi offers a peaceful retreat from the city's energy, with opportunities for hiking, cycling, and visiting traditional craft villages. These excursions make Hanoi not just a destination, but a starting point for broader exploration of Vietnam's northern regions.

4.2 Must-See Attractions

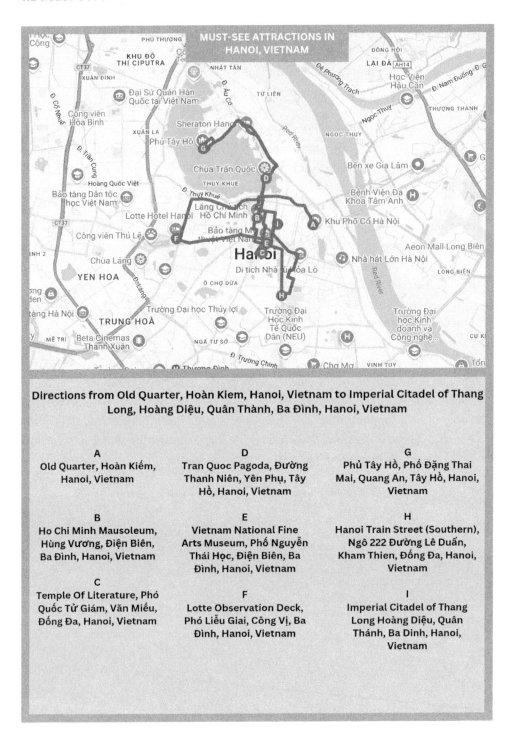

Directions from Old Quarter, Hoàn Kiem, Hanoi, Vietnam to Imperial Citadel of Thang Long, Hoàng Diệu, Quân Thành, Ba Đình, Hanoi, Vietnam

A
Old Quarter, Hoàn Kiếm, Hanoi, Vietnam

B
Ho Chi Minh Mausoleum, Hùng Vương, Điện Biên, Ba Đình, Hanoi, Vietnam

C
Temple Of Literature, Phó Quốc Tử Giám, Văn Miếu, Đống Đa, Hanoi, Vietnam

D
Tran Quoc Pagoda, Đường Thanh Niên, Yên Phụ, Tây Hồ, Hanoi, Vietnam

E
Vietnam National Fine Arts Museum, Phố Nguyễn Thái Học, Điện Biên, Ba Đình, Hanoi, Vietnam

F
Lotte Observation Deck, Phó Liễu Giai, Cống Vị, Ba Đình, Hanoi, Vietnam

G
Phủ Tây Hồ, Phố Đặng Thai Mai, Quang An, Tây Hồ, Hanoi, Vietnam

H
Hanoi Train Street (Southern), Ngõ 222 Đường Lê Duẩn, Kham Thien, Đống Đa, Hanoi, Vietnam

I
Imperial Citadel of Thang Long Hoàng Diệu, Quân Thánh, Ba Dinh, Hanoi, Vietnam

4.2.1 Old quarters

Located in the heart of Vietnam's capital, Hanoi, the Old Quarters is an iconic district steeped in history, culture, and a bustling vibrancy that captures the essence of the city. For any visitor looking to experience the authentic charm of Hanoi, the Old Quarters is a must-see destination. Its narrow streets, historical architecture, and unique local life make it an enchanting area that offers more than just a glimpse into Vietnam's rich past.

Location and Getting There
The Old Quarters is conveniently situated just north of Hoàn Kiếm Lake, one of Hanoi's most famous landmarks. The district is well-connected by various modes of transportation, making it easy for visitors to access. If you are staying in central Hanoi, walking is the most enjoyable way to enter the Old Quarters. You'll find that the intricate web of streets, filled with shops, cafes, and historical sites, starts to unfold before you. If you prefer a quicker option, taxis, ride-hailing services, or motorbikes can take you to the district in no time. For those coming from farther away, the Old Quarters is only about a 45-minute drive from Nội Bài International Airport. Many hotels in Hanoi also offer shuttle services, making the journey even more convenient. Public buses run frequently, and they stop near major entry points to the Old Quarters.

Entry Fee

One of the many advantages of visiting the Old Quarters is that there is no entry fee. The streets and markets are open to all, allowing visitors to explore the area freely. However, some individual historical sites within the district, such as ancient temples or museums, may charge a small fee for entry. It is advisable to carry some local currency (Vietnamese Dong) for such instances.

Why It Is Worth Visiting

The Old Quarters is a treasure trove of Vietnamese culture, history, and local life. Walking through its maze of streets feels like stepping back in time to the days of ancient Hanoi. The district retains its original layout from centuries ago, with streets named after the goods they were historically associated with, such as Hang Bac (Silver Street) or Hang Gai (Silk Street). This unique characteristic sets the Old Quarters apart from other modernized districts in the city, offering an authentic, nostalgic atmosphere. Beyond the historical layout, the Old Quarters is a place where old meets new. Traditional shop houses and temples stand alongside trendy cafes and boutiques, creating an intriguing mix of past and present. For those seeking to experience Vietnam's living culture, the Old Quarters is the perfect place to do so. You can observe the daily lives of locals, taste street food, and shop for handmade crafts and souvenirs that reflect Hanoi's artistry.

Historical and Cultural Significance

The Old Quarters dates back over a thousand years, making it one of the oldest urban areas in Southeast Asia. It was originally a commercial hub where skilled artisans from various parts of Vietnam would come to sell their wares. The district was organized around craft guilds, with each street specializing in a particular trade, such as metalworking, silk weaving, or herbal medicine. Over time, these streets became known by their craft names, which remain to this day. The area is also home to many important historical sites, such as the Bach Ma Temple, one of the oldest temples in Hanoi, and the Dong Xuan Market, a bustling local market that has operated since the 19th century. The Old Quarters offers insight into the architectural styles that have shaped Hanoi, from traditional Vietnamese designs to French colonial influences that arrived in the 19th and early 20th centuries. Walking through the Old Quarters feels like wandering through a living museum, with every corner telling a story of the city's past.

What to Do in the Old Quarters

There is no shortage of things to do in the Old Quarters. One of the best ways to experience the area is simply by walking through its narrow, winding streets. Each street offers something different, from souvenir shops selling traditional lacquerware and silk scarves to local eateries serving famous Vietnamese dishes like pho and banh mi. Visitors can spend hours exploring the markets, such as Dong Xuan Market, which is the largest indoor market in Hanoi. Here, you can find everything from fresh produce and spices to clothes and electronics. The market offers a unique glimpse into the daily life of Hanoi's residents and is the perfect place to pick up gifts or try local snacks. Cultural landmarks like Bach Ma Temple, located on Hang Buom Street, provide a peaceful retreat from the lively streets. This temple is dedicated to the white horse, which, according to legend, helped guide the construction of the city's walls. Visitors can take in the serene atmosphere and admire the temple's intricate architecture, offering a moment of reflection amidst the hustle and bustle. Food lovers will delight in the endless variety of street food available in the Old Quarters. Hanoi is renowned for its street cuisine, and the Old Quarters is at the heart of this culinary tradition. You can try everything from a steaming bowl of pho to sweet and savory spring rolls. Be sure to visit local cafes and try Vietnamese egg coffee, a unique and delicious treat made from whipped egg yolks and coffee. At night, the Old Quarters transform into a vibrant nightlife destination. The area around Ta Hien Street, also known as "Beer Street," comes alive with locals and tourists alike, enjoying the open-air bars and lively atmosphere. It's the perfect place to unwind after a day of sightseeing, mingle with locals, and enjoy the city's vibrant energy.

Other Information Visitors Need to Know

When visiting the Old Quarters, it's important to be prepared for the lively, chaotic energy of the area. The streets can get crowded, especially during weekends and holidays, so it's best to wear comfortable shoes and be ready for a lot of walking. The district's narrow lanes are best navigated on foot or by bike, as cars and large vehicles are often too cumbersome for the area. If you're visiting during the hotter months, be sure to carry water and wear a hat or sunscreen, as the midday heat can be intense. There are many cafes and restaurants where you can take a break and cool off, so feel free to pop into a local spot for a refreshing drink. For those interested in learning more about the history of the Old Quarters, guided tours are available. Many local companies offer walking tours that delve deeper into the area's history, architecture, and culture, providing a richer experience for visitors. Lastly, although the Old Quarters is a safe area, it's always wise to keep an eye on your belongings, as pickpocketing can occasionally happen in crowded tourist areas. Being aware of your surroundings ensures a safe and enjoyable visit.

4.2.2 Ho Chi Minh Mausoleum

Nestled in the heart of Hanoi, the Ho Chi Minh Mausoleum stands as a monumental tribute to one of Vietnam's most revered figures, Ho Chi Minh, the founding father of modern Vietnam. This grandiose mausoleum, which houses the preserved body of "Uncle Ho," as he is affectionately called, offers visitors a profound glimpse into Vietnam's revolutionary history and serves as a pilgrimage site for those who hold Ho Chi Minh's legacy dear. For any traveler visiting Hanoi, this is a must-see attraction that provides both a moving historical experience and a connection to Vietnam's past.

Location and How to Get There
The Ho Chi Minh Mausoleum is situated in the Ba Dinh District of Hanoi, on the edge of Ba Dinh Square, a significant political and cultural hub. Ba Dinh Square itself is historically important, as it was here that Ho Chi Minh declared the independence of Vietnam in 1945.

Getting to the mausoleum is relatively easy. If you are staying in the Old Quarter of Hanoi, you can either take a short taxi ride or, for a more immersive experience, walk or cycle through the bustling streets of Hanoi to arrive at the site. Public buses also service the area with stops close to the mausoleum. Alternatively, using ridesharing apps like Grab can ensure a convenient and affordable ride to the site.

Entry Fee and Visiting Hours
One of the unique aspects of the Ho Chi Minh Mausoleum is that entry is free, making it accessible to all visitors who wish to learn more about Vietnam's history. However, visitors should be mindful of the mausoleum's operating hours. It is typically open from 7:30 AM to 10:30 AM, with closures on Mondays and Fridays. The mausoleum is closed annually for maintenance from September to November, so planning your visit around these times is essential.

Why It Is Worth Visiting
Visiting the Ho Chi Minh Mausoleum is not just about seeing the resting place of a prominent leader—it is about stepping into a place where history, culture, and national pride converge. For the Vietnamese, the mausoleum is a place of reverence and respect, and for tourists, it offers a deep insight into the sacrifices made by the people of Vietnam in their quest for independence. The solemn atmosphere of the mausoleum, coupled with the grandeur of its architecture, makes the visit a moving experience. The mausoleum itself is an architectural marvel, influenced by Lenin's Mausoleum in Moscow, but with unique Vietnamese touches. It's built from materials sourced across Vietnam, symbolizing the unity of the nation under Ho Chi Minh's leadership. Surrounding the mausoleum is a peaceful, immaculately maintained garden, which offers a tranquil escape from the busy city streets of Hanoi.

Historical and Cultural Significance
Ho Chi Minh is considered the founding father of modern Vietnam. His role in leading the country through its struggles for independence from French colonial rule and his vision of a unified Vietnam have made him an enduring symbol of national pride. The mausoleum serves as a reminder of his contributions, standing as a permanent monument to his ideals of independence, freedom, and unity. The preservation of his body inside the mausoleum is symbolic of the people's desire to keep him close, even in death. Visiting this site allows you to witness firsthand how deeply ingrained Ho Chi Minh's legacy is in Vietnamese

culture. Furthermore, it highlights the people's respect for their history and their leaders, giving visitors a broader perspective on Vietnam's national identity.

What to Do There

Once inside the mausoleum, visitors are guided in a respectful, orderly line past Ho Chi Minh's glass-encased body. The atmosphere inside is hushed, with guards ensuring the sanctity of the space. This part of the visit is brief but powerful, allowing for quiet reflection on the man who shaped Vietnam's future. After viewing the body, visitors can explore the surrounding area, which includes several other notable attractions. The Presidential Palace, where Ho Chi Minh worked and lived, lies nearby and offers a fascinating glimpse into his personal life. The humble stilt house, where he chose to reside instead of the opulent palace, reflects his modest lifestyle and his connection to the common people. Adjacent to these is the Ho Chi Minh Museum, where exhibitions delve deeper into his life, his works, and the history of Vietnam's fight for independence. Visitors should also take a stroll around Ba Dinh Square and visit the iconic One Pillar Pagoda, a symbol of Vietnam's rich Buddhist tradition. The pagoda is located within walking distance from the mausoleum, making it a convenient addition to your visit.

Practical Information for Visitors

When visiting the mausoleum, it's essential to dress appropriately out of respect for the site's solemnity. Modest attire is required—knees and shoulders should be covered, and hats must be removed upon entering the mausoleum. Visitors are also prohibited from taking photographs inside the mausoleum, and speaking loudly or using mobile phones is discouraged to maintain the respectful atmosphere. Queues can form early in the morning, especially on weekends or national holidays, so it's advisable to arrive early to avoid long waiting times. Security is tight, and visitors will have their bags scanned before entering the mausoleum complex. It is worth noting that there is a formal and dignified tone to the visit, which adds to the overall experience of paying respects to one of the most influential figures in Vietnam's history.

4.2.3 Temple of Literature

Located in the heart of Hanoi, the Temple of Literature stands as a symbol of Vietnam's rich educational and cultural heritage. This ancient site, founded in 1070 during the reign of Emperor Ly Thanh Tong, was originally dedicated to Confucius and later became the country's first national university. The temple is a must-see for anyone visiting Hanoi, offering an immersive experience into Vietnam's traditional architecture, history, and intellectual values.

Location and How to Get There
The Temple of Literature is conveniently located about 2 kilometers west of Hoan Kiem Lake, at 58 Quốc Tử Giám Street, in the Dong Da district. It is easily accessible from Hanoi's Old Quarter by taxi, motorbike, or even a leisurely walk if you wish to explore the surrounding streets. Many visitors choose to visit the temple as part of a day tour, often pairing it with other nearby attractions.

Entry Fee and Visiting Hours
The entrance fee to the Temple of Literature is approximately 30,000 VND (about 1.25 USD), making it an affordable stop for travelers. The temple is open from 8:00 AM to 5:00 PM, though visitors are advised to check for possible changes in schedule during holidays or special events. Early mornings or late

afternoons are ideal times to visit, as the temple can get crowded during peak hours.

Why It's Worth Visiting

The Temple of Literature is more than just an architectural marvel; it's a journey through Vietnam's intellectual history. As you step through the imposing gates, you'll be greeted by beautiful courtyards, tranquil ponds, and stone-carved steles that commemorate the scholars who passed the rigorous imperial exams. The atmosphere is serene, offering a quiet reprieve from Hanoi's bustling streets.

The temple is also a place of reverence, with many locals and students visiting to pray for success in their studies. The blend of Confucian principles with Vietnamese traditions gives the site a unique cultural significance, making it a fascinating place for both history enthusiasts and those seeking a deeper understanding of Vietnamese spirituality.

Historical and Cultural Significance

The Temple of Literature holds profound historical and cultural importance as the birthplace of higher education in Vietnam. In the early years of the Lý Dynasty, the temple was not only a place for worship but also the site of the Imperial Academy, Vietnam's first national university. Here, scholars were trained in the Confucian classics, and the rigorous imperial exams were held to select the country's most promising students for high-ranking government positions. The temple's five courtyards, arranged in a symmetrical layout, are each designed to represent different aspects of the journey toward wisdom and enlightenment. The Well of Heavenly Clarity and the pavilion housing the Stelae of Doctors are among the most significant features, where the names of those who passed the prestigious exams are inscribed in stone.

What to Do and See at the Temple of Literature

Visitors can explore the tranquil courtyards, admire the traditional Vietnamese architecture, and view ancient artifacts on display. The Well of Heavenly Clarity, a large rectangular pond, offers a picturesque setting, while the pavilions and altars dedicated to Confucius and his disciples provide insights into the spiritual importance of the site. Art lovers will enjoy the vibrant Vietnamese calligraphy workshops often held within the temple grounds, where skilled artisans create beautiful scrolls that make for meaningful souvenirs. During the Lunar New

Year, the temple becomes particularly lively, as students come to ask for blessings of good luck in their studies.

Additional Tips for Visitors
Be sure to dress modestly when visiting the temple, as it is considered a sacred site. Comfortable shoes are recommended, as there's a fair amount of walking involved. The temple's location near Hanoi's Old Quarter also makes it easy to combine your visit with other iconic attractions, such as the Ho Chi Minh Mausoleum or the One Pillar Pagoda.

4.2.4 Ha Long Bay

If the Temple of Literature is a testament to Vietnam's cultural and intellectual heritage, then Ha Long Bay is a reflection of its stunning natural beauty. Located roughly 170 kilometers from Hanoi, Ha Long Bay is a UNESCO World Heritage Site renowned for its emerald waters and towering limestone karsts. For any visitor to Hanoi, a trip to Ha Long Bay is an absolute must, offering a striking contrast to the city's historic sites and vibrant streets.

Location and How to Get There
Ha Long Bay is situated in Quang Ninh Province, on the northeastern coast of Vietnam. From Hanoi, the most convenient way to reach Ha Long Bay is by bus, shuttle, or private car, with the journey taking approximately 2.5 to 4 hours

depending on traffic and the mode of transportation. Many tour operators in Hanoi offer full-day or overnight trips to Ha Long Bay, often including hotel pickup and drop-off, as well as boat cruises that explore the bay's most scenic spots.

Entry Fee and Cruise Options
The entry fee to Ha Long Bay varies depending on the route and type of cruise you choose. Basic entrance tickets to the bay are around 290,000 VND (about 12 USD). However, most visitors opt for a boat tour, which can range from budget-friendly day trips to luxurious overnight cruises. Prices for these tours start at around 500,000 VND (about 21 USD) for a day tour and can go up significantly for more elaborate multi-day cruises that include accommodation and meals.

Why Ha Long Bay is Worth Visiting
Ha Long Bay's landscape is nothing short of magical. Thousands of limestone islands and islets rise dramatically from the emerald waters, forming a surreal seascape that looks like something out of a fantasy novel. The bay's natural beauty has earned it a spot on many travelers' bucket lists, and rightfully so. The tranquility of floating on the calm waters, surrounded by towering rock formations, offers a profound sense of peace and awe. Whether you're a nature lover, photographer, or simply someone looking to unwind in one of the world's most beautiful settings, Ha Long Bay is an experience you won't soon forget.

Historical and Cultural Significance
Ha Long Bay is not just a natural wonder but also a place rich in history and folklore. According to legend, the bay was created by dragons sent by the gods to protect Vietnam from invaders. The dragons are said to have spat out jewels and jade, which formed the bay's iconic limestone islands. Historically, Ha Long Bay has been inhabited for thousands of years, with archaeological sites revealing the existence of prehistoric cultures that once thrived in the area. Today, the bay is home to several fishing communities who live in floating villages, preserving traditional ways of life that visitors can observe and appreciate.

What to Do and See in Ha Long Bay
A cruise through Ha Long Bay is the best way to experience its beauty. Visitors can explore hidden caves, kayak through crystal-clear waters, or swim on

secluded beaches. One of the most popular stops is Sung Sot (Surprise) Cave, a vast cavern filled with stalactites and stalagmites, offering breathtaking views from its entrance. For those interested in adventure, Ha Long Bay provides ample opportunities for rock climbing and hiking on Cat Ba Island, the largest island in the bay. Many cruises also offer visits to local fishing villages, where visitors can learn about the daily lives of the bay's residents and try their hand at traditional fishing methods.

Additional Tips for Visitors

If you're planning to stay overnight, booking a cruise that offers cabins with bay views is highly recommended for a truly immersive experience. Make sure to bring sunscreen, as the sun can be quite strong during the day, and pack a light jacket for cooler evenings on the water. While Ha Long Bay is beautiful year-round, the best time to visit is from October to April when the weather is cooler and the skies are clearer.

4.3 Hidden Gems of Hanoi

Hanoi is renowned for its rich history, stunning architecture, and bustling streets filled with the intoxicating aromas of street food. While the popular attractions such as Hoan Kiem Lake and the Old Quarter capture the hearts of many, hidden within the city are gems waiting to be discovered. These lesser-known spots offer a glimpse into the authentic essence of Hanoi, showcasing its culture, creativity, and charm away from the tourist crowds. Each hidden gem tells a unique story, providing visitors with experiences that linger long after their visit.

Trấn Quốc Pagoda

Nestled on a small island in the serene waters of West Lake, Trấn Quốc Pagoda is a stunning Buddhist sanctuary that exudes tranquility and beauty. Established in the sixth century, it is one of the oldest pagodas in Vietnam and features a striking red-and-gold color scheme that stands out against the lush greenery surrounding it. As you wander through the ornate entrance, you'll be greeted by the soft sounds of chanting and the fragrance of incense wafting through the air. The pagoda is adorned with intricately carved statues and lotus flowers, creating a peaceful atmosphere that invites contemplation and reflection. Visitors can take a leisurely stroll around the lake, absorbing the picturesque views of the pagoda reflected in the water, especially at sunset when the golden hues paint the sky, making it an idyllic spot for photography.

The Vietnam National Fine Arts Museums

Located in a beautifully restored French colonial villa, the Vietnam National Fine Arts Museum is a hidden treasure that showcases the country's rich artistic heritage. The museum features an extensive collection of both traditional and contemporary Vietnamese art, with works ranging from ancient sculptures to modern paintings. Each exhibit tells a story, reflecting the cultural evolution and historical experiences of Vietnam. As you explore the museum's galleries, take your time to appreciate the intricate details of the artworks, including traditional lacquer paintings and folk art that highlight the creativity of Vietnamese artisans. The museum also hosts temporary exhibitions that introduce visitors to emerging artists, offering a dynamic insight into Vietnam's contemporary art scene. With fewer crowds compared to other attractions, this museum provides a peaceful haven for art enthusiasts and curious travelers alike.

Lotte Observation Deck

For a breathtaking panoramic view of Hanoi, the Lotte Observation Deck is an excellent hidden gem that often goes unnoticed by visitors. Located on the 65th floor of the Lotte Center Hanoi, this observation deck offers a stunning vista of the city skyline and the sprawling landscape beyond. Ascend to the top in a high-speed elevator, and as you step out, you'll be greeted with sweeping views that stretch as far as the eye can see. The sunset here is particularly mesmerizing, as the city transforms into a sea of lights, casting a magical glow over the streets below. Whether you choose to visit during the day or at night, the Lotte Observation Deck is a perfect spot for both relaxation and inspiration. Don't forget your camera, as the stunning backdrop is ideal for capturing memorable moments.

Phu Tay Ho

Phu Tay Ho, or Tay Ho Temple, is a lesser-known spiritual site located on the banks of West Lake. This serene temple complex is dedicated to the worship of the goddess of fertility, making it a popular spot for locals seeking blessings for family and children. As you approach the temple, you'll be enveloped by the lush greenery and the calming sounds of nature, creating an atmosphere of peace and spirituality. The main temple features intricate sculptures and beautifully painted frescoes, depicting the goddess and various deities. Visitors can join locals in prayer and offerings, gaining insight into the spiritual practices of the Vietnamese people. The tranquil surroundings make it an ideal place to escape the hustle and bustle of the city and immerse oneself in the cultural and religious traditions of Hanoi.

The Hanoi Train Street

Hanoi's Train Street is a quirky and fascinating hidden gem that offers a glimpse into the daily life of locals living alongside the railway tracks. Here, you can witness the unique phenomenon of trains passing through narrow alleyways just inches away from homes and cafés. As the train approaches, residents swiftly move their belongings to make way for the locomotive, showcasing the incredible adaptability and resilience of the Vietnamese people. This vibrant street is lined with charming cafés and eateries, where you can sip coffee while watching the trains go by. The atmosphere is electric, as the sound of the train horn blends with the chatter of locals and the aroma of freshly brewed Vietnamese coffee. A visit to Train Street is a must for those seeking an authentic and exhilarating experience that captures the essence of Hanoi's urban life.

The Imperial Citadel of Thang Long

While many travelers flock to the bustling streets of Hanoi, the Imperial Citadel of Thang Long remains a hidden historical gem that tells the story of Vietnam's past. This UNESCO World Heritage Site dates back to the 11th century and served as the political center of Vietnam for nearly a millennium. Visitors can explore the remnants of ancient walls, gates, and palaces that have withstood the test of time. The archaeological site reveals layers of history, showcasing the cultural influences that have shaped Vietnam throughout the centuries. As you wander through the grounds, take a moment to appreciate the stunning architecture and the serene gardens that offer a peaceful escape from the city's noise. The citadel also houses a museum that provides valuable insights into the historical significance of the site, making it a perfect destination for history enthusiasts.

Hanoi's Hidden Cafés

Venturing off the beaten path, Hanoi's hidden cafés provide a delightful experience for coffee lovers looking to immerse themselves in the local culture. Tucked away in quaint alleyways and residential areas, these charming spots often feature unique themes and cozy atmospheres, offering a warm escape from the hustle and bustle of the city. One such hidden gem is a traditional Vietnamese coffee shop where you can savor a cup of rich, strong coffee brewed using a traditional phin filter. Here, the aroma of roasted beans mingles with the sounds of laughter and conversation, creating a warm and inviting ambiance. Many of these cafés also serve delectable local pastries and snacks, allowing you to indulge in the flavors of Vietnam while mingling with friendly locals. Exploring these hidden cafés not only tantalizes your taste buds but also gives you a glimpse into the daily lives of Hanoi's residents.

4.4 Exploring Hanoi's Neighborhoods

French Quarter

The French Quarter of Hanoi is a stark contrast to the Old Quarter's chaotic energy. Here, visitors can experience the elegance and grandeur of French colonial architecture, with wide tree-lined boulevards, stately buildings, and a more tranquil atmosphere. Located southeast of Hoan Kiem Lake, the French Quarter is home to some of the city's most important landmarks, including the Hanoi Opera House and the Presidential Palace. Walking through this neighborhood feels like stepping back in time to the days when Hanoi was a key part of French Indochina, with a European aesthetic that is still evident in its grand facades and quiet avenues. This area is ideal for those looking to enjoy a more leisurely pace while still immersing themselves in the history and culture of the city. Visitors can explore iconic landmarks, visit museums such as the Vietnam National Museum of History, or relax in one of the many chic cafes that line the streets. The French Quarter is also known for its upscale dining options, offering some of the finest restaurants in the city. Whether taking in a performance at the opera house or simply enjoying a peaceful afternoon walk, the French Quarter offers a different perspective on Hanoi's rich cultural tapestry.

Tay Ho

Tay Ho, also known as West Lake, is one of Hanoi's most scenic and tranquil neighborhoods, offering a peaceful escape from the busier parts of the city. Located to the north of Hanoi, Tay Ho surrounds the city's largest lake, providing stunning views and a laid-back atmosphere. This neighborhood has become a popular area for both locals and expats, with its blend of modern conveniences and natural beauty. The serene lakeside setting is perfect for leisurely strolls, and visitors can often see locals fishing, practicing tai chi, or simply enjoying the view from one of the many cafes that dot the lakeside. Tay Ho is known for its international dining scene, with a variety of restaurants offering global cuisine, from Italian to Indian, catering to the city's expatriate community. The neighborhood is also home to some of Hanoi's most luxurious hotels and resorts, making it an ideal destination for those seeking both relaxation and comfort. Visitors can explore cultural landmarks like the ancient Tran Quoc Pagoda, one of the oldest in the city, or visit one of the many art galleries showcasing local and international artists. Whether renting a bicycle to ride around the lake or simply enjoying a sunset by the water, Tay Ho offers a serene contrast to the bustling city center.

Ba Dinh

Ba Dinh is the political heart of Hanoi and is home to some of the most important historical and governmental buildings in Vietnam. This neighborhood, located west of the Old Quarter, is where visitors will find the Ho Chi Minh Mausoleum, a monumental site that holds the embalmed body of the country's revolutionary leader. Surrounding the mausoleum are beautifully landscaped gardens and the iconic Ba Dinh Square, where Ho Chi Minh declared Vietnam's independence in 1945. This neighborhood is steeped in national pride and historical significance, making it an essential stop for visitors interested in Vietnam's modern history. Beyond its political importance, Ba Dinh is also home to several cultural sites, including the One Pillar Pagoda and the Vietnam Military History Museum. Visitors can explore these landmarks and gain a deeper understanding of the country's struggle for independence and its cultural heritage. The area also offers a quieter atmosphere compared to the Old Quarter, with wide boulevards and leafy streets perfect for a relaxing stroll. Ba Dinh's blend of history, politics, and culture provides a comprehensive look at both Hanoi's past and present, making it an integral part of any visit to the city.

Truc Bach

Tucked away near West Lake, Truc Bach is one of Hanoi's lesser-known neighborhoods, offering visitors an authentic glimpse of local life away from the tourist crowds. This charming neighborhood, centered around the peaceful Truc Bach Lake, is perfect for those looking to explore Hanoi at a slower pace. The area is filled with cozy cafes, traditional Vietnamese eateries, and quiet streets where life moves at a more relaxed rhythm. Truc Bach's small, winding streets are home to a variety of hidden gems, from local street food vendors to small temples that offer a moment of serenity. One of the highlights of Truc Bach is its culinary scene, with some of the best local dishes in Hanoi, including the famous pho cuon, a type of fresh spring roll unique to the area. Visitors can enjoy a meal by the lake while watching the sunset or explore the narrow streets

54

that reveal a mix of old and new architecture. Truc Bach's proximity to both West Lake and the Old Quarter makes it an ideal base for exploring the city, while still offering a quiet retreat from the bustling streets. This neighborhood is perfect for those looking to experience a more authentic side of Hanoi, where the local culture thrives.

4.5 Dining and Nightlife in Hanoi

Ngon Villa

Ngon Villa, located in the heart of Hanoi's French Quarter, offers a dining experience that encapsulates the diversity of Vietnamese cuisine. This restaurant takes visitors on a culinary journey across the regions of Vietnam, with dishes that highlight the flavors of the north, center, and south. Ngon Villa is renowned for its family-style dining, where guests can sample a wide array of traditional dishes, including fresh spring rolls, succulent grilled meats, and aromatic noodle soups. The ambiance of the restaurant is both cozy and elegant, with traditional Vietnamese décor creating a warm, inviting atmosphere. Ngon Villa opens its doors in the late morning and serves into the evening, making it a perfect spot for both lunch and dinner. The restaurant also offers a wide selection of beverages, from local Vietnamese beers to imported wines, complementing the flavorful dishes on offer. Guests can indulge in classic Vietnamese desserts to round off their meal, such as sweet sticky rice with mango or banana pudding. Whether dining with friends, family, or even alone, Ngon Villa promises an unforgettable dining experience that highlights the best of Vietnamese culinary traditions. Its central location makes it easy to access, while its authentic dishes ensure that visitors leave with a deeper appreciation for the country's food culture.

The Deck Saigon

The Deck Saigon, nestled along the banks of the Saigon River, offers a sophisticated dining experience in the vibrant city of Ho Chi Minh. This upscale restaurant is famed for its fusion of Vietnamese and international flavors, creating a unique menu that caters to both locals and tourists. The Deck's riverside location provides stunning views, particularly at sunset when the city lights begin to shimmer across the water. Guests can enjoy dishes like fresh seafood, perfectly grilled steaks, and inventive vegetarian options, all prepared with the finest local ingredients. The restaurant is open from mid-morning until late at night, offering lunch, dinner, and a stylish cocktail bar that comes alive after dark. The Deck is not only a place for fine dining but also a popular nightlife spot, with a carefully curated drinks menu that includes exotic cocktails, fine wines, and premium spirits. Its chic, open-air design allows diners to enjoy the tropical breeze while savoring their meals, making it an ideal venue for special occasions or romantic dinners. Visitors can expect top-tier service and an atmosphere of understated luxury, where the combination of exceptional food and a scenic setting creates an unforgettable experience. Whether for a lavish meal or a quiet drink by the water, The Deck Saigon offers a perfect escape from the bustling city.

Tạ Hiện Street

For those seeking an authentic and lively nightlife experience, Tạ Hiện Street in Hanoi's Old Quarter is the place to be. Known as the "Beer Street" among locals and tourists alike, this vibrant neighborhood is famous for its bustling atmosphere, affordable drinks, and street-side eateries. As the sun sets, Tạ Hiện transforms into a lively hub where locals and visitors gather to enjoy bia hơi, Vietnam's famous draft beer, alongside plates of grilled meats, fried spring rolls, and other street food favorites. The street comes alive with music, laughter, and the clinking of glasses, creating an electric atmosphere that perfectly captures Hanoi's energetic nightlife. Tạ Hiện Street's charm lies in its unpretentious vibe and the sense of community it fosters among its patrons. Visitors can grab a stool at one of the many makeshift bars, order a cold beer, and immerse themselves in the street's vibrant energy. The eateries here stay open well into the early morning hours, ensuring that night owls have plenty of time to soak in the experience. While the street food is simple, it's packed with flavor and offers a perfect pairing with the cheap, refreshing beer. For those looking to experience Hanoi's nightlife in its purest form, a visit to Tạ Hiện Street is a must.

Skylight Nha Trang

Skylight Nha Trang, located atop one of the city's tallest buildings, offers visitors an unparalleled dining and nightlife experience with breathtaking views of the coastline. This rooftop bar and restaurant are known for its stunning 360-degree views of Nha Trang Bay, the city skyline, and the surrounding mountains. The menu at Skylight is a fusion of international and Vietnamese cuisine, featuring fresh seafood, gourmet burgers, and handcrafted cocktails. Visitors can dine in style while taking in the spectacular sunset, or they can head to the bar area later in the evening to dance the night away under the stars. Skylight's nightlife scene is a major draw for both locals and tourists, with live DJ sets and themed parties creating a vibrant atmosphere that lasts into the early hours of the morning. The venue's chic, modern design, combined with its panoramic views, makes it one of Nha Trang's premier nightlife destinations. Skylight also offers a diverse drinks menu, with everything from classic cocktails to locally inspired creations that showcase the flavors of Vietnam. Whether you're there for a romantic dinner or a night of dancing, Skylight provides an unforgettable experience that blends fine dining with a lively nightlife scene.

Xu Bar

Xu Bar, located in the heart of District 1 in Ho Chi Minh City, is the epitome of modern Vietnamese dining and sophisticated nightlife. The venue is split into two levels, with the ground floor serving as a contemporary restaurant offering innovative takes on traditional Vietnamese dishes. Guests can enjoy delicacies such as caramelized pork belly, lotus root salads, and fresh seafood, all prepared with a modern twist. Xu Bar prides itself on using the finest ingredients to create dishes that honor Vietnam's culinary heritage while incorporating global flavors. The restaurant opens for lunch and dinner, providing a stylish yet relaxed atmosphere for guests to enjoy their meals. As night falls, Xu transforms into a trendy bar and lounge, attracting a fashionable crowd with its expertly crafted cocktails, premium spirits, and chic décor. The bar area, located upstairs, is designed for those looking to enjoy a more intimate and upscale nightlife experience. With its dim lighting, plush seating, and soft music, Xu Bar offers a refined escape from the city's bustling streets. Whether you're in the mood for a quiet drink or an elegant meal, Xu provides a seamless blend of dining and nightlife, making it a must-visit destination for those looking to experience the modern side of Ho Chi Minh City.

Broma

For a more relaxed and intimate nightlife experience, Broma: Not a Bar offers a rooftop oasis in the heart of Ho Chi Minh City. This casual bar is known for its laid-back vibe, offering visitors a chance to enjoy craft beers, signature cocktails, and light snacks while taking in the city's skyline. Located just a short walk from the iconic Ben Thanh Market, Broma is a hidden gem that attracts both locals and expats looking for a chilled evening out. The bar's cozy rooftop setting is perfect for unwinding after a long day of sightseeing, with live music and DJ performances adding to the laid-back ambiance. Broma is open from the early evening until late at night, offering a refuge from the city's fast-paced energy. Visitors can enjoy a range of locally brewed beers or opt for one of the bar's creative cocktails, many of which incorporate traditional Vietnamese ingredients. The atmosphere is casual and friendly, making it a great spot to meet fellow travelers or simply relax with friends. For those looking to escape the louder, more crowded parts of the city's nightlife scene, Broma offers a peaceful and welcoming environment where good drinks and good company are the main focus.

CHAPTER 5
DISCOVERING NORTHERN VIETNAM

5.1 Overview of Northern Vietnam

Northern Vietnam is a region that embodies the essence of the country's landscapes, traditions, and history. From the towering mountains and lush valleys to the bustling cities and quiet villages, it offers a diverse experience for any traveler seeking both adventure and cultural immersion. Known for its stunning natural wonders, unique ethnic communities, and vibrant history, northern Vietnam presents an opportunity to explore the heart and soul of a country that is as captivating as it is complex.

Geography and Climate of Northern Vietnam
The geography of northern Vietnam is dominated by dramatic mountain ranges, lush river valleys, and dense forests. This region stretches from the flat plains of the Red River Delta in the east to the towering peaks of the Hoàng Liên Son range in the northwest. In between are vast expanses of rice paddies, rolling hills, and remote villages nestled deep within the countryside. The region's most iconic natural landmark is Ha Long Bay, a UNESCO World Heritage Site where thousands of limestone karsts rise from the emerald waters, creating an ethereal

seascape that seems straight out of a dream. The climate in northern Vietnam is subtropical with four distinct seasons. Spring and autumn offer the most pleasant weather, with mild temperatures and lower humidity. Summers, which run from May to August, can be hot and humid, with heavy monsoon rains often visiting the region. Winter, especially in the mountainous areas like Sapa, can be surprisingly cold, with occasional frost in the higher elevations. For travelers, the best time to visit largely depends on the experience they seek, whether it's the cool misty winters or the lush green landscapes of the rainy season.

Cultural Significance and Ethnic Diversity

Northern Vietnam is not just rich in natural beauty; it is also home to a vibrant and diverse cultural tapestry. The region is known for its ethnic minority groups, such as the Hmong, Dao, Tay, and Thai, each with their own languages, customs, and traditional clothing. These groups have lived in the mountains and valleys for centuries, maintaining their unique way of life despite the passage of time. Visitors to northern Vietnam have the rare opportunity to interact with these communities, learn about their crafts, and experience their customs firsthand. The villages of northern Vietnam, particularly around Sapa and Ha Giang, offer a glimpse into a world where life has changed little over the years. Traditional farming methods, intricate handwoven textiles, and ancient rituals are still very much a part of daily life. For those seeking authentic cultural experiences, spending time with these communities, whether through a homestay or village visit, is both humbling and enriching.

The Historical Heart of Vietnam

Northern Vietnam holds deep historical significance for the country. Hanoi, the bustling capital, is the cultural and political heart of Vietnam, with a history that dates back over a thousand years. The Old Quarter of Hanoi, with its narrow streets and French colonial architecture, is a living testament to the city's rich history, where ancient temples and pagodas coexist with modern cafés and bustling markets. The city is home to many key historical sites, including Ho Chi Minh's Mausoleum, the Temple of Literature, and the ancient One Pillar Pagoda. For history lovers, Hanoi is a treasure trove of stories and landmarks that offer insight into Vietnam's complex past. Further north, the region is also known for its role in the country's more recent history. The northern mountains were a stronghold during the struggle for independence, with many areas playing key roles during the First Indochina War and the Vietnam War. War memorials, museums, and historic battlefields can be found throughout the region, allowing visitors to connect with the country's tumultuous journey towards reunification and independence.

Natural Wonders That Dazzle the Senses

Northern Vietnam is a paradise for nature lovers and adventure seekers. Ha Long Bay, with its mystical islands and hidden caves, is perhaps the most famous destination in the region. Cruising through the bay, either on a traditional junk boat or kayak, provides an otherworldly experience as you navigate through a maze of towering limestone formations. While Ha Long Bay is a popular destination, the lesser-known Bai Tu Long Bay offers a quieter, more tranquil alternative for those looking to avoid the crowds. The far northern province of Ha Giang is another natural marvel, with its rugged mountain terrain and remote landscapes. Known for its breathtaking loop road, Ha Giang offers some of the most stunning vistas in Vietnam. Travelers will pass through misty mountain passes, deep river valleys, and terraced rice fields that stretch for miles. This is a place where nature reigns supreme, and every turn in the road reveals a new view that seems even more beautiful than the last. In addition to the dramatic mountains and bays, northern Vietnam is also home to lush national parks, such as Ba Be National Park and Cuc Phuong National Park. These parks are teeming with wildlife, dense forests, and stunning waterfalls. Ba Be Lake, the largest natural freshwater lake in Vietnam, is located within Ba Be National Park and offers a serene escape where visitors can explore by boat or kayak, surrounded by limestone cliffs and verdant forests.

Adventure and Exploration in Northern Vietnam

For those seeking adventure, northern Vietnam provides ample opportunities for trekking, biking, and exploring. The town of Sapa, located in the Hoàng Liên Son mountains, is one of the top trekking destinations in the region. From here, visitors can embark on multi-day treks through terraced rice fields, past waterfalls, and up into the misty mountains. Whether you're a seasoned hiker or just looking for a day trek, the landscape around Sapa is nothing short of spectacular. Fansipan, the highest mountain in Vietnam, is a challenging climb, but for those not inclined to hike, a cable car now whisks visitors to the summit for panoramic views. Other adventurous activities include motorbiking through the remote mountain passes of Ha Giang or kayaking in the peaceful inlets of Ha Long Bay. Whether on foot, bike, or boat, northern Vietnam invites exploration at every turn.

The Local Cuisine of Northern Vietnam

No visit to northern Vietnam is complete without indulging in the region's rich culinary heritage. Northern Vietnamese cuisine is distinct from the flavors found in the central and southern parts of the country. The dishes here are influenced by the cooler climate and the abundance of local herbs, rice, and vegetables. Phở, the world-famous noodle soup, originates from Hanoi, and there's no better place to try an authentic bowl than in the capital's bustling street markets. Other must-try dishes include bun cha (grilled pork with noodles), cha ca (turmeric fish with dill), and xôi (sticky rice). The food in northern Vietnam is typically lighter and less spicy than in the south, with an emphasis on fresh ingredients and balanced flavors. Visitors will find no shortage of street vendors, markets, and restaurants offering mouth-watering local specialties.

Practical Information for Visitors

Travelers to northern Vietnam will find a range of accommodations, from budget-friendly hostels to luxurious hotels. In the cities, there are numerous options to suit all tastes and budgets, while in the rural areas, homestays provide a more authentic and immersive experience. English is widely spoken in the more tourist-heavy areas, but in the more remote regions, some knowledge of basic Vietnamese or the help of a local guide may be necessary. When traveling in northern Vietnam, it's essential to pack for varying weather conditions, particularly if visiting the mountains where temperatures can drop significantly, especially at night. Comfortable walking shoes, rain gear, and layers are recommended, as are sun protection and insect repellent. For transportation, Vietnam has an extensive bus and train network connecting most major cities and towns. Overnight trains from Hanoi to destinations such as Sapa or Lào Cai are a popular and scenic way to travel. Motorbike rentals are also a common choice for travelers looking to explore at their own pace.

5.2 Must-See Attractions

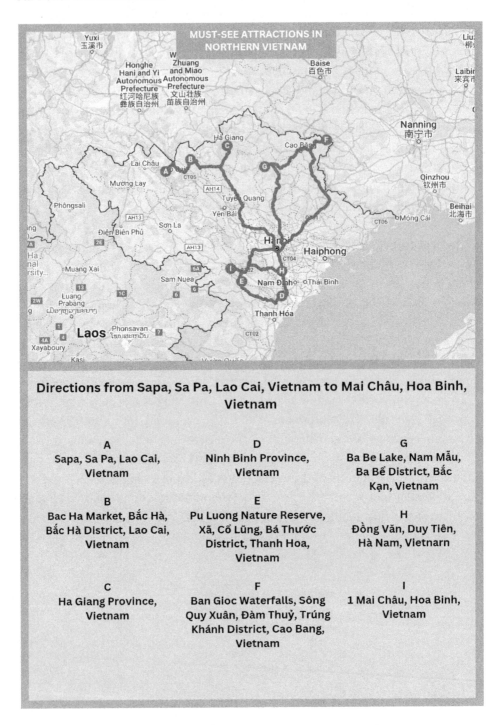

5.2.1 Sapa Town

Tucked away in the breathtaking mountains of northern Vietnam, Sapa Town is a destination that feels like stepping into a painting. The region, known for its spectacular landscapes, terraced rice fields, and rich cultural diversity, is more than just a pretty backdrop—it is a place that will stay with you long after you leave. A must-see for travelers seeking both adventure and serenity, Sapa Town is a gateway to exploring the raw beauty of Vietnam's northern highlands.

Where is Sapa Located?
Sapa Town is located in Lào Cai Province, a mountainous area in the far northwest of Vietnam. Nestled at an altitude of 1,600 meters (5,250 feet), Sapa enjoys a temperate climate, providing a cool and refreshing escape from Vietnam's often sweltering heat. Surrounded by the Hoàng Liên Son mountain range, including Vietnam's highest peak, Fansipan, Sapa feels like a hidden paradise embraced by clouds.

How to Get There
Most visitors begin their journey to Sapa from Hanoi, the capital of Vietnam. The most popular route is via an overnight train or bus to Lào Cai City, which takes about 8 to 10 hours. From Lào Cai, it's an additional hour-long drive by

bus, taxi, or private car up the winding roads to Sapa Town. For those seeking a quicker option, there are also luxury shuttle buses that travel directly from Hanoi to Sapa, making the trip in about 5 to 6 hours.

Entry Fee and Accessibility
There is no entry fee to visit Sapa Town itself, but some attractions, such as the Fansipan cable car or visits to local villages, may have small fees. Many of the hikes, markets, and scenic spots around Sapa are accessible for free, making it a budget-friendly destination for nature lovers and adventurers alike. It's advisable to carry cash for local purchases, as ATM availability can be limited in the more rural areas surrounding the town.

Why Sapa is Worth Visiting
Sapa Town is worth visiting because it is a perfect blend of stunning landscapes and deep cultural roots. Its iconic terraced rice paddies cascade down the slopes like giant green steps, while misty mountains create an ethereal backdrop that changes with the seasons. In spring, flowers bloom across the valley, in summer the rice terraces gleam emerald, in autumn they turn golden, and winter brings a cool, almost frosty ambiance. But beyond its natural beauty, Sapa is also a cultural treasure. The town is home to various ethnic minority groups, such as the Hmong, Dao, Tay, and Giay, each with their own distinct traditions, clothing, and way of life. A visit to Sapa is an opportunity to not only appreciate nature but also to immerse yourself in the lives of the people who have called this land home for generations.

Historical and Cultural Significance
Sapa has a long history that intertwines with the colonial past of Vietnam. It was first established as a French hill station in the early 20th century, serving as a retreat for French administrators seeking cooler weather. This colonial influence can still be seen in some of the old French villas scattered around the town, lending it a quaint European charm amidst the Vietnamese highlands. However, the true heart of Sapa lies in its ethnic minority communities. These groups have lived in the region for centuries, cultivating the land and preserving their unique cultures. Each village around Sapa has its own identity, and visitors can witness traditional farming methods, embroidery, and even take part in local festivals. The town's cultural tapestry is as rich and diverse as its landscapes, making it a place where every corner holds a story.

What to Do in Sapa

Sapa offers an array of activities that cater to all types of travelers. For outdoor enthusiasts, trekking is the most popular activity. There are numerous trails leading through the hills, offering stunning views of rice terraces, bamboo forests, and mountain peaks. Many treks include visits to local villages such as Cat Cat, Ta Van, and Lao Chai, where you can meet the Hmong and Dao people, learn about their customs, and even stay in homestays for an authentic experience. One of the highlights of any trip to Sapa is the journey to the top of Fansipan, known as the "Roof of Indochina." At 3,143 meters (10,312 feet), Fansipan is the highest mountain in Vietnam, and while climbing it is a challenging multi-day trek, the cable car offers a more accessible way to reach the summit. From the top, you'll be rewarded with sweeping views of the Hoàng Liên Son range and the valleys below. For those interested in local culture, the weekend markets in Sapa Town are a must-visit. The most famous is the Bac Ha Market, which takes place on Sundays and attracts people from all over the region. Here, you'll find everything from handmade textiles and silver jewelry to local produce and livestock. The market is also a vibrant cultural exchange, with different ethnic groups coming together to trade, socialize, and celebrate.

Other Information Visitors Need to Know

The best time to visit Sapa depends on what kind of experience you're looking for. If you want to see the rice terraces at their greenest, the ideal time is between May and September. However, this is also the rainy season, and trails can become muddy and slippery. October and November offer cooler, drier weather with golden rice fields ready for harvest. Winter months, from December to February, bring mist and frost, and while the views may be limited by the fog, the atmosphere feels magical. When packing for Sapa, it's important to bring layers, as temperatures can vary dramatically, especially if you're trekking. Comfortable hiking shoes, rain gear, and sun protection are also essential. While Sapa Town has a range of accommodation options, from budget hostels to luxury hotels, staying in a village homestay can provide a deeper connection to the local culture. As for food, Sapa is known for its hearty, mountain-style cuisine. Dishes like thang co (a traditional Hmong stew), grilled meats, and sticky rice are popular, and many restaurants also serve hotpots to warm up on cooler evenings. Don't miss the chance to try locally grown produce like peaches, plums, and herbal teas, which are sold in the markets and by roadside vendors.

5.2.2 Bac Ha Market

Bac Ha Market is a captivating destination nestled in the mountainous region of northern Vietnam. For those seeking an authentic, immersive experience, this market offers a window into the daily lives and rich traditions of the region's ethnic minorities. Known for its vibrant colors, unique handicrafts, and bustling energy, Bac Ha Market is more than just a place of commerce; it is a celebration of culture and history. This iconic market, held every Sunday, is one of the largest in the region, drawing visitors from all over Vietnam and the world.

Location and How to Get There
Bac Ha Market is located in Bac Ha town, in the Lao Cai Province of northern Vietnam. The town sits approximately 100 kilometers northeast of Sapa, a popular destination known for its scenic beauty and trekking opportunities. Most visitors come to Bac Ha as a day trip from Sapa, which is a 2.5 to 3-hour drive through picturesque mountains and valleys. For those starting their journey in Hanoi, Bac Ha is about a 7-hour drive, or visitors can take a train or bus to Lao Cai city and then a connecting bus or taxi to Bac Ha. There are no entry fees to visit Bac Ha Market, but transportation costs vary depending on the mode of travel. Many visitors opt for guided tours from Sapa or Hanoi, which typically include transportation, a guide, and sometimes meals.

Why Bac Ha Market Is Worth Visiting

Bac Ha Market is a cultural treasure that showcases the diversity of northern Vietnam's ethnic minority communities. It is the largest market in the area, attracting people from all around the region who come to trade goods, livestock, handicrafts, and produce. The market is particularly famous for the colorful attire of the Flower Hmong people, who are known for their vibrant, hand-embroidered clothing. Visiting Bac Ha Market is an opportunity to witness an authentic local tradition that has been preserved for generations. The market offers a rare glimpse into the daily lives of the Hmong, Tay, and Phu La people, among others. Beyond its commercial function, Bac Ha Market is a social hub where families and friends gather to catch up, share meals, and celebrate their cultural heritage. For travelers seeking an experience that goes beyond the typical tourist attractions, Bac Ha Market is a must-visit. It is a place where tradition and commerce intersect, offering visitors a deeper understanding of the region's people and their way of life.

Historical and Cultural Significance

Bac Ha Market has deep historical roots in northern Vietnam. For centuries, the market has served as a vital trading post for the region's ethnic minorities, allowing them to exchange goods, livestock, and produce with one another. Over time, the market has become more than just a place of commerce—it has become a cultural symbol of the region's ethnic diversity and resilience. The market plays an important role in preserving traditional craftsmanship, especially among the Flower Hmong. Many of the goods sold at the market, such as textiles, clothing, and jewelry, are handmade using techniques passed down through generations. Visitors can purchase these unique handicrafts, knowing that their money is supporting the local artisans and their cultural heritage. In addition to its cultural significance, Bac Ha Market also holds historical importance. The market has witnessed the evolution of the region over time, adapting to the changing political and economic landscape of Vietnam while maintaining its traditional charm. For locals, Bac Ha Market is not only a place to buy and sell goods but also a place to maintain their cultural identity in an ever-changing world.

What to Do at Bac Ha Market

A visit to Bac Ha Market is an immersive experience that engages all the senses. From the moment you arrive, you will be greeted by a whirlwind of sights, sounds, and smells. The market is divided into different sections, each offering a

68

unique glimpse into the region's diverse offerings. One of the most fascinating areas is the livestock market, where local farmers trade cattle, pigs, horses, and buffalo. This section is particularly lively, as farmers haggle over prices and inspect the animals on display. Even if you're not in the market for livestock, it's worth wandering through this area to observe the energy and excitement. The handicraft section is another highlight of Bac Ha Market. Here, you can find beautifully handcrafted textiles, jewelry, and clothing made by the region's ethnic minorities. The vibrant colors and intricate patterns of the Flower Hmong's clothing are especially eye-catching. Many visitors purchase these items as souvenirs or gifts, knowing they are supporting the local economy. For food lovers, Bac Ha Market is a paradise. The food section is filled with vendors selling fresh produce, spices, and traditional Vietnamese dishes. Don't miss the opportunity to try local delicacies such as thang co, a traditional soup made from horse meat, which is a specialty of the region. If horse meat doesn't appeal to you, there are plenty of other options, including sticky rice, grilled meats, and fresh fruits. Bac Ha Market is also a great place for photography enthusiasts. The vibrant colors of the market, the bustling crowds, and the dramatic backdrop of the mountains create the perfect setting for capturing stunning images. Whether you're an amateur or professional photographer, you'll find plenty of inspiration here.

Other Information a Visitor Needs to Know

Bac Ha Market is best visited early in the morning when the market is most lively, and you can catch the vendors setting up their stalls. Arriving early also allows you to experience the market before the crowds of tourists arrive. The market typically winds down by early afternoon, so plan your visit accordingly. Although English is not widely spoken at the market, the locals are friendly and welcoming to visitors. A few basic Vietnamese phrases, such as "xin chào" (hello) and "cảm ơn" (thank you), can go a long way in making connections with the vendors. For those interested in extending their visit, Bac Ha town has a few accommodation options, ranging from budget guesthouses to mid-range hotels. Staying overnight in Bac Ha allows you to explore the surrounding area, including the Ban Pho village, known for its traditional Hmong houses and corn wine production. Visitors should also note that Bac Ha Market is only held on Sundays, so plan your trip accordingly. If you're traveling to Bac Ha as part of a longer journey through northern Vietnam, consider combining your visit with a trip to nearby attractions such as Sapa, the Hoang Lien Son mountain range, or the Ban Ho Valley.

5.2.3 Ha Giang Province

Nestled in the far north of Vietnam, Ha Giang Province is an unspoiled gem that has captivated adventurous travelers and culture seekers alike. Famous for its dramatic landscapes, vibrant local cultures, and raw beauty, Ha Giang remains one of Vietnam's most authentic travel destinations. Offering a rugged terrain of limestone peaks, lush valleys, and winding roads, the province embodies the spirit of untouched natural beauty combined with deep-rooted traditions. For those who seek the road less traveled, Ha Giang presents a truly extraordinary experience.

Location and How to Get There

Ha Giang Province is situated in the northernmost part of Vietnam, bordering China. It lies about 300 kilometers (186 miles) from Hanoi, making it a perfect destination for those looking to explore the rural and scenic landscapes of the region. Travelers can reach Ha Giang from Hanoi by taking a bus or hiring a motorbike, with the bus journey taking approximately 7-8 hours. Buses depart daily from My Dinh Bus Station in Hanoi, offering both day and night options. For the adventurous, traveling by motorbike provides an exhilarating experience, giving the opportunity to enjoy the views along the way and explore at your own pace.

Why Ha Giang is Worth Visiting

The allure of Ha Giang lies in its sheer isolation and unspoiled nature. Unlike many tourist-heavy destinations, Ha Giang offers a genuine experience of rural life, ethnic minority cultures, and jaw-dropping natural beauty. Visitors can expect towering limestone mountains, terraced rice fields that cascade down steep hillsides, and deep river gorges that cut through the landscape. Its roads, often precariously winding through mountain passes, offer some of the most scenic views in all of Vietnam. Ha Giang's quiet charm is in its authenticity—the welcoming smiles of locals, the daily rhythms of village life, and the harmonious coexistence with nature.

The Historical and Cultural Significance

Ha Giang is home to a diverse array of ethnic minority groups, including the Hmong, Tay, and Dao people. These communities have lived in the region for centuries, preserving ancient customs, traditional dress, and unique ways of life. The historical significance of the area is deeply intertwined with these ethnic cultures. The province's distinctive architecture, colorful markets, and festivals reflect a rich cultural tapestry, largely untouched by modernity. Ha Giang's past also includes a strategic role during various conflicts, including the Vietnam War and border disputes with China. Visitors can gain a deeper understanding of the province's history by engaging with local guides or visiting historical sites.

What to Do in Ha Giang

The top activity in Ha Giang is undoubtedly exploring the majestic landscape, either by motorbike or car. The *Ha Giang Loop* is a renowned motorbike route that takes visitors through a 350-kilometer loop of steep mountain passes, plunging valleys, and rural villages. Highlights of the loop include the Ma Pi Leng Pass, considered one of the most breathtaking roads in Southeast Asia, and the Dong Van Karst Plateau, a UNESCO Global Geopark famous for its karst formations and geological wonders. For those seeking cultural immersion, visiting the local markets, such as Dong Van and Meo Vac, provides a vivid glimpse into the daily lives of the ethnic minority communities. Trekking is another popular activity in Ha Giang. With trails that weave through rice terraces and villages, visitors can enjoy a more intimate connection with the natural surroundings. Local homestays offer a unique experience to stay with ethnic families, share traditional meals, and learn about local customs firsthand. The Lung Cu Flag Tower, located at Vietnam's northernmost point, is another must-see, offering panoramic views and a symbol of the country's unity and strength.

Entry Fees and Practical Information

There is no general entry fee for visiting Ha Giang Province; however, certain attractions may require a small fee. For example, visiting the Lung Cu Flag Tower typically requires a fee of around 20,000 VND (less than 1 USD), while motorbike rentals for the Ha Giang Loop range from 150,000-250,000 VND per day (6-10 USD). Visitors should also be aware that Ha Giang's roads can be challenging, particularly for those unfamiliar with motorbike travel. It is advised to travel with a guide or join a tour if safety is a concern. The best time to visit Ha Giang is during the dry season, from October to April, when the weather is cooler and the skies are clearer. The region's terraced rice fields are especially beautiful in September and October, during harvest time. For those interested in local festivals, visiting during the lunar new year (Tet) or the Hmong ethnic group's New Year celebrations in December can provide a fascinating cultural experience.

Cultural Etiquette and What to Know Before You Go

As a remote and culturally rich area, it is important for visitors to respect the local customs and traditions in Ha Giang. When visiting ethnic villages, it is always a good idea to dress modestly and ask for permission before taking photographs, especially of people. Many locals still live in traditional houses, and entering these homes should be done with respect. Small gifts, such as snacks or toys for children, are often appreciated, but avoid giving money directly to children as it can disrupt the local culture. Learning a few basic phrases in Vietnamese, or even better, in the local languages of the ethnic groups, can go a long way in fostering goodwill. Guides and homestay hosts are often happy to share insights into their way of life, so don't hesitate to ask questions and engage in conversations.

Why Ha Giang Should Be on Your List

Ha Giang Province offers an unparalleled experience for those looking to explore the raw, untamed beauty of northern Vietnam. With its dramatic landscapes, vibrant ethnic cultures, and rich history, it stands as a must-see destination for travelers who seek authenticity and adventure. The roads that cut through its towering mountains are not for the faint-hearted, but the reward lies in the awe-inspiring views, the warm hospitality of its people, and the sense of connection to a place still untouched by the fast pace of modern life. For anyone eager to experience the "real Vietnam"—where nature remains wild and traditions remain alive—Ha Giang is the answer. Whether it's riding the famous loop, trekking through ancient rice terraces, or spending a night in a hilltop village, this province will leave an indelible mark on your heart. Pack your sense of adventure, prepare for winding roads, and let Ha Giang show you a side of Vietnam that few have the chance to see.

5.2.4 Ninh Binh Province

Ninh Binh Province, nestled in northern Vietnam, stands as one of the country's most breathtaking and diverse destinations. Known for its stunning limestone karst landscapes, tranquil rivers, historical sites, and rich culture, Ninh Binh is often referred to as "Ha Long Bay on land." Whether you're an avid nature lover, a history enthusiast, or a seeker of peaceful, off-the-beaten-path experiences, Ninh Binh has something for everyone. From the towering mountains to the ancient temples, this province offers visitors a mesmerizing blend of natural beauty and cultural depth, making it a must-see destination in Vietnam.

Location and How to Get There
Ninh Binh is located around 100 kilometers south of Hanoi, making it an easy and convenient escape from the hustle and bustle of the capital. Travelers can access Ninh Binh by train, bus, or private vehicle from Hanoi, with the journey

taking about two hours by car. The province is well-connected via Highway 1, and regular buses and trains depart from Hanoi's Giap Bat and My Dinh bus stations, as well as from Hanoi Railway Station. Alternatively, for those looking for a more relaxed and scenic journey, private car services and motorbike rentals are popular options that allow for flexible exploration of the countryside.

Why Ninh Binh is Worth Visiting
Ninh Binh is often overlooked by tourists who are drawn to the more popular Ha Long Bay, but this province offers a quieter, more immersive experience. Its dramatic landscapes are dominated by towering limestone mountains rising out of the verdant rice paddies and winding rivers, creating a setting that feels otherworldly. Beyond the natural beauty, the area holds a deep historical and cultural significance, with ancient temples, pagodas, and caves waiting to be explored. Whether you're paddling through the peaceful waters of Tam Coc or visiting the historic capital of Hoa Lu, Ninh Binh offers a rare combination of stunning scenery and rich heritage that is hard to match elsewhere in Vietnam.

Historical and Cultural Significance
Ninh Binh has a long and storied history, being the site of Vietnam's ancient capital, Hoa Lu. During the Dinh and Le dynasties, Hoa Lu served as the political, economic, and cultural center of the country in the 10th and 11th centuries. Today, visitors can explore the remnants of this ancient capital, including temples dedicated to the former emperors and fortifications that once protected the kingdom from invasion. These historical sites provide a fascinating insight into the beginnings of the Vietnamese nation, with a strong connection to the country's cultural and spiritual heritage. In addition to its historical significance, Ninh Binh is home to some of the most revered religious sites in Vietnam. Bai Dinh Pagoda, the largest pagoda complex in Southeast Asia, draws thousands of pilgrims each year. Its stunning architecture, combined with its spiritual significance, makes it an essential stop for visitors interested in Vietnam's religious traditions. The peaceful atmosphere of the pagoda complex, set against a backdrop of towering mountains, creates an unforgettable experience for visitors.

What to Do in Ninh Binh
For those looking to immerse themselves in the natural beauty of Ninh Binh, there are a multitude of activities that will leave you breathless. Tam Coc, often referred to as the "Three Caves," is one of the most popular attractions in the

area. Visitors can take a peaceful boat ride along the Ngo Dong River, passing through limestone caves and between towering karst cliffs. The boat journey through Tam Coc is often likened to a slow, serene glide through another world, as the water reflects the dramatic rock formations and lush green fields surrounding the riverbanks. Trang An Landscape Complex, a UNESCO World Heritage site, offers a similar but even more expansive experience, with its intricate network of rivers, caves, and temples. A boat ride here takes visitors through a labyrinth of waterways and hidden grottoes, revealing historical temples and shrines along the way. For those interested in trekking, Mua Cave is a must-visit. The hike to the top of Hang Mua mountain rewards visitors with panoramic views of the surrounding countryside, including Tam Coc and the sprawling rice fields below. The sight from the summit, particularly at sunset, is nothing short of magical, with the lush, green landscape stretching out as far as the eye can see. Another key historical site to visit is Hoa Lu Ancient Capital, where visitors can wander through the remains of the old city walls, temples, and relics. This site is a treasure trove for history buffs, offering insights into the dynastic period of Vietnam. The area is not only historically significant but also incredibly picturesque, surrounded by dramatic landscapes that add to the allure of the experience.

Entry Fees and Additional Information

Entry fees for the main attractions in Ninh Binh are relatively modest. A boat tour through Tam Coc costs around 120,000 VND (approximately $5 USD), while Trang An boat tours range from 150,000 to 200,000 VND (about $6-$8 USD). Mua Cave requires a small entrance fee of around 100,000 VND (around $4 USD), and visitors can access Hoa Lu for a fee of 20,000 VND (under $1 USD). Bai Dinh Pagoda, being a religious site, is free to enter, though there is a small fee for the electric car service to reach the pagoda complex. Visitors should note that the best time to visit Ninh Binh is during the dry season, from November to April, when the weather is cooler and more comfortable for outdoor activities. The rainy season, from May to October, can make some of the roads and pathways slippery and difficult to navigate, though the region is still accessible.

Why Ninh Binh Should Be on Every Traveler's Itinerary

Ninh Binh offers an unparalleled experience in northern Vietnam, combining natural beauty, cultural depth, and historical significance. It is a place where visitors can feel connected to the country's past, while also enjoying the tranquility of its stunning landscapes. The province's slow pace, compared to the bustling streets of Hanoi, allows visitors to fully absorb the beauty of the area and experience Vietnam's rural life up close. Whether you are rowing through the emerald rivers, hiking up the limestone cliffs, or exploring ancient temples, Ninh Binh offers moments of serenity and reflection. The sheer diversity of experiences—ranging from historical exploration to spiritual journeys and natural adventures—ensures that every visitor leaves with lasting memories of this enchanting province. For anyone seeking an authentic and unspoiled corner of Vietnam, Ninh Binh is a destination that should not be missed.

5.3 Hidden Gems of Northern Vietnam

Pu Luong Nature Reserve

Pu Luong Nature Reserve is a hidden gem tucked away in the lush mountains of Thanh Hoa province, offering a peaceful retreat for those seeking an authentic connection with nature. This serene reserve is home to terraced rice fields, misty valleys, and ethnic minority villages, providing a window into traditional Vietnamese rural life. Visitors can trek through the stunning landscapes, explore remote villages, and witness the timeless beauty of the rice terraces that ripple across the hillsides. The area's cooler climate and unspoiled nature make it an ideal escape from the bustling cities, inviting travelers to slow down and immerse themselves in the tranquil surroundings. Getting to Pu Luong from Hanoi takes about four hours by car, but the scenic drive through the countryside is an adventure in itself. Upon arrival, visitors can stay in charming eco-lodges or homestays, where they can enjoy the hospitality of the local Thai and Muong ethnic groups. The accommodations are simple yet comfortable, allowing travelers to experience a more rustic and grounded side of Vietnam. The best time to visit is during the rice harvesting season, when the fields glow a golden yellow under the soft sunlight. For those who love outdoor activities, trekking and cycling through the reserve offer unparalleled views of the natural landscape, while more adventurous souls can explore the impressive waterfalls and caves that dot the area.

Ban Gioc Waterfall

Located on the border between Vietnam and China, Ban Gioc Waterfall is one of the most awe-inspiring natural wonders in northern Vietnam. The waterfall cascades down in multiple tiers, creating a dramatic curtain of water that plunges into the Quay Son River, with limestone cliffs towering above. The sight of the falls, with their thunderous roar and misty spray, is nothing short of breathtaking, and the surrounding landscape of emerald rice paddies and karst mountains only adds to the enchantment. As one of the largest waterfalls in Southeast Asia, Ban Gioc is not just a visual spectacle but also a symbol of the natural beauty that defines the region. Visitors can take a boat ride to the base of the falls, where they can feel the refreshing mist on their faces and witness the raw power of the cascading water up close. The area around Ban Gioc is relatively quiet, with fewer tourists than other famous attractions, making it the perfect destination for those seeking solitude in nature. While in the area, travelers can also visit the nearby Nguom Ngao Cave, a stunning limestone cave filled with stalactites and stalagmites, or explore the charming villages of the Tay and Nung ethnic groups. The journey to Ban Gioc from Hanoi takes around seven hours, but the scenic route through rolling hills and ethnic communities is worth the effort.

Ba Be Lake

Ba Be Lake, located in Bac Kan province, is another hidden gem in northern Vietnam that captivates visitors with its tranquil beauty. Nestled in the heart of Ba Be National Park, this freshwater lake is surrounded by dense forests, towering limestone mountains, and charming minority villages. The still waters of the lake reflect the surrounding landscape like a mirror, creating a serene and almost magical atmosphere. Ba Be is perfect for those looking to escape into nature and enjoy activities like kayaking, boat trips, or hiking through the park's lush jungle trails. The lake is also home to several ethnic minority communities, including the Tay and Dao people, who live in traditional stilt houses along the water's edge. Staying in a homestay offers visitors a chance to learn about the local culture and experience the warm hospitality of the villagers. Ba Be National Park is rich in biodiversity, with an abundance of wildlife, including rare birds, primates, and butterflies. Visitors can take a boat ride to explore hidden caves, such as Puong Cave, or enjoy a leisurely day fishing or swimming in the pristine waters. The journey to Ba Be from Hanoi takes around five hours by car, and the peaceful, off-the-beaten-path experience makes it a rewarding destination for nature lovers.

Dong Van Karst Plateau

The Dong Van Karst Plateau, located in Ha Giang province, is a UNESCO Global Geopark that offers visitors an unforgettable experience of Vietnam's rugged northern highlands. This dramatic landscape is characterized by its towering limestone peaks, deep valleys, and traditional hill tribe villages, creating a picture-perfect setting that feels untouched by time. The plateau is home to various ethnic minority groups, including the Hmong, Tay, and Lo Lo people, whose colorful traditional clothing and vibrant markets add to the region's cultural richness. Travelers can embark on one of Vietnam's most scenic road trips along the Ha Giang Loop, which winds through the plateau and offers breathtaking views at every turn. Along the way, visitors can stop in villages, trek through the karst landscapes, or visit historical sites such as the Hmong King's Palace. The best time to visit is during the buckwheat flower season, when the hills are blanketed in delicate pink blooms, creating a truly magical scene. Dong Van Karst Plateau is a journey into Vietnam's cultural and natural heritage, where the landscapes are as timeless as the traditions of the people who call it home.

Mai Chau

Mai Chau, located just a few hours southwest of Hanoi, is a hidden gem that offers a peaceful and idyllic escape into Vietnam's rural heartland. Surrounded by green valleys, rice fields, and limestone mountains, Mai Chau is home to the White Thai ethnic group, whose traditional stilt houses and way of life provide a charming contrast to the hustle and bustle of urban life. The valley is a haven of tranquility, where visitors can take leisurely bike rides through rice paddies, enjoy traditional dance performances, and sample the delicious local cuisine. Mai Chau is particularly beautiful in the late afternoon, when the sun casts a golden glow over the rice fields and the mountains in the distance. The area offers a range of activities for travelers, from trekking to exploring nearby caves, but it's also the perfect place to simply relax and soak in the peaceful surroundings. Homestays in traditional wooden houses provide an authentic experience, and visitors are often invited to join their hosts for meals and cultural exchanges. The journey from Hanoi to Mai Chau takes about three hours, making it an easy and rewarding day trip or overnight getaway from the city. Each of these hidden gems in northern Vietnam offers a unique glimpse into the country's natural beauty and cultural richness. From the serene waters of Ba Be Lake to the majestic Ban Gioc Waterfall, the rugged landscapes of Dong Van Plateau to the peaceful rice fields of Mai Chau, these destinations invite travelers to explore a side of Vietnam that remains untouched by mass tourism. For those looking to venture off the beaten path, northern Vietnam's hidden gems offer unforgettable experiences, where nature, culture, and tradition come together in perfect harmony.

5.4 Trekking and Homestays

Vietnam's stunning landscapes offer the perfect backdrop for trekking adventures combined with immersive homestay experiences. For those looking to explore the country's natural beauty, trekking through Vietnam's lush mountains and valleys, while staying in traditional homes, is an unforgettable way to connect with the culture and the land. Visitors will not only experience Vietnam's breathtaking scenery but also have the opportunity to engage with local communities. These homestays offer comfort and authenticity, providing a unique and enriching experience that goes beyond the typical tourist path.

Sapa

Sapa, located in northern Vietnam, is renowned for its terraced rice fields and vibrant ethnic communities, making it one of the most popular trekking destinations in the country. Trekking through Sapa's lush green hills offers visitors the chance to pass through traditional villages, interact with the Hmong people, and experience their way of life firsthand. Many homestays in Sapa, such as the Ta Van village homestay, offer cozy accommodations with prices ranging around $10 to $20 per night. These homestays are often located in the heart of the mountains, providing a perfect base for exploring the surrounding trails. To access Sapa, visitors can take an overnight train or bus from Hanoi, which takes approximately 6-8 hours. Once in Sapa, local guides often lead trekking tours that include overnight stays in village homestays, where guests can enjoy homemade meals prepared by their hosts. Trekking in Sapa offers not only stunning views but also a glimpse into the daily lives of the ethnic minority groups that inhabit the region. The combination of physical adventure and cultural immersion makes Sapa a must-visit destination for trekking enthusiasts.

Mai Chau

Mai Chau, located southwest of Hanoi, offers a more peaceful trekking experience, with gentle valleys, lush rice paddies, and traditional stilt houses dotting the landscape. Trekking in Mai Chau is less strenuous than in Sapa, making it ideal for those seeking a more relaxed adventure. Visitors can stay in homestays such as the Mai Chau Ecolodge, where prices range from $20 to $30 per night. These homestays are built in the traditional style of the local White Thai ethnic group, providing a unique opportunity to live like a local while enjoying modern comforts. Getting to Mai Chau from Hanoi is easy, with buses taking about four hours to reach the destination. Once there, visitors can embark on guided treks that lead them through picturesque villages and peaceful valleys.

The slower pace of life in Mai Chau offers visitors the chance to unwind and fully appreciate the natural beauty of the region. Homestays in Mai Chau often include meals made from locally sourced ingredients, offering a true farm-to-table experience. The combination of serene trekking routes and cultural immersion makes Mai Chau a hidden gem for travelers.

Ha Giang

Ha Giang, located in the far north of Vietnam, is one of the most remote and rugged regions of the country, offering challenging treks through dramatic mountain landscapes. Trekking in Ha Giang takes visitors through deep valleys, towering limestone peaks, and remote ethnic villages, providing a raw and authentic trekking experience. Homestays in Ha Giang, such as those in Dong Van or Meo Vac, typically range from $15 to $25 per night and offer simple but comfortable accommodations. Staying with local families provides visitors with the chance to learn about the traditions of the Hmong, Tay, and Dao ethnic groups. To access Ha Giang, travelers can take an overnight bus from Hanoi, which takes about 8-10 hours. Once in Ha Giang, visitors can arrange guided treks with local experts who know the terrain intimately. Trekking through Ha Giang offers a sense of adventure and discovery, as many of the trails are less traveled by tourists. The region's rugged beauty and the warm hospitality of its people make Ha Giang an ideal destination for those looking for an off-the-beaten-path trekking experience. The cultural richness of the area adds an extra layer of depth to the trekking journey.

Pu Luong Nature Reserve

Pu Luong Nature Reserve, located near Mai Chau, offers an eco-friendly trekking experience through one of Vietnam's most pristine natural areas. The reserve is home to dense forests, waterfalls, and terraced rice fields, providing a stunning backdrop for trekkers. Homestays in Pu Luong, such as the Pu Luong Retreat, offer eco-friendly accommodations with prices around $30 to $40 per night. These homestays are designed to blend seamlessly with the natural environment, offering visitors a chance to disconnect from the hustle and bustle of city life. Pu Luong is accessible by bus from Hanoi, with the journey taking approximately five hours. Once in the reserve, visitors can embark on guided treks that take them through remote villages and untouched landscapes. Staying in a homestay in Pu Luong offers a chance to experience rural life in Vietnam, with local families providing traditional meals and warm hospitality. The emphasis on eco-tourism in Pu Luong ensures that visitors can enjoy the beauty

80

of the region while minimizing their environmental impact. The combination of natural beauty and sustainable tourism makes Pu Luong a must-visit destination for eco-conscious travelers.

Bac Ha

Bac Ha, located northeast of Sapa, is famous for its colorful ethnic markets and scenic trekking routes that take visitors through the region's rolling hills and lush valleys. Trekking in Bac Ha offers a quieter alternative to the more touristy areas of northern Vietnam, with fewer crowds and more opportunities to explore the region's natural beauty. Homestays in Bac Ha, such as those in the Ban Pho village, typically cost between $10 and $15 per night, offering simple yet comfortable accommodations. Visitors staying in these homestays can enjoy home-cooked meals and learn about the customs of the Flower Hmong people. Bac Ha is accessible by bus from Sapa or Lao Cai, with the journey taking about three hours. The region's ethnic markets, held on weekends, are a highlight for visitors, offering a chance to witness the vibrant culture of the local communities. Trekking through Bac Ha's scenic landscapes and staying in a traditional homestay provides an authentic experience that showcases the rich cultural heritage of the region. The peaceful atmosphere and stunning natural beauty make Bac Ha an ideal destination for those seeking both adventure and cultural immersion.

CHAPTER 6
EXPLORING CENTRAL VIETNAM

6.1 Overview of Central Vietnam

Central Vietnam is a region brimming with cultural richness, natural beauty, and historical depth, offering travelers a captivating and multifaceted experience. This region, known for its coastal landscapes, verdant mountains, ancient towns, and imperial cities, is a journey into the heart of Vietnam's storied past and vibrant present. Stretching along the coast between the north and the south, Central Vietnam is a perfect destination for those seeking both adventure and tranquility, with its combination of history, beaches, and rural charm.

A Diverse Geographical Landscape

Central Vietnam is known for its diverse landscapes, ranging from pristine beaches to majestic mountain ranges. The long stretch of coastline offers some of Vietnam's most beautiful beaches, including the famous white sands of Da Nang and the quiet, less crowded shores of Quy Nhon. These coastal areas are perfect for relaxation, swimming, and water sports, while the warm, crystal-clear waters of the South China Sea offer an inviting retreat for beach lovers. Further inland, the Annamite Mountains rise up, with lush greenery and misty peaks that beckon nature enthusiasts and trekkers. These mountains also house ancient tribal communities that live in harmony with nature, adding a unique cultural dimension to the region's natural beauty. The picturesque Hai Van Pass, a scenic mountain road connecting Da Nang and Hue, provides some of the most breathtaking views in all of Vietnam, with its steep climbs and sweeping vistas of the sea and countryside.

Historical and Cultural Treasures

Central Vietnam is a region steeped in history, from ancient Champa ruins to the imperial grandeur of the Nguyen Dynasty. Hue, the former capital of imperial Vietnam, is home to the famous Hue Imperial City, a UNESCO World Heritage Site that offers a glimpse into the royal past of the country. Walking through its gates and palaces, visitors can feel the echoes of Vietnam's emperors and their grand ceremonies. Hue is also known for its royal tombs and pagodas, which dot the landscape and reflect the reverence for both the living and the dead in Vietnam's royal history. Further south, the ancient town of Hoi An offers a well-preserved example of a Southeast Asian trading port from the 15th to the 19th century. Its charming streets, lined with lanterns and historical houses, evoke a romantic, timeless atmosphere. Hoi An is not only famous for its architecture but also for its culinary heritage, offering some of the best food experiences in the country. The town's riverside location, coupled with its bustling markets, makes it a vibrant, yet peaceful, destination for cultural immersion. Da Nang, a modern city known for its beaches and vibrant nightlife, also holds historical significance. It is home to the Marble Mountains, a cluster of five marble and limestone hills, each representing one of the five elements. Visitors can explore caves, temples, and pagodas while taking in panoramic views of the surrounding area. Da Nang also serves as a gateway to the ancient kingdom of My Son, where the remains of Hindu temples built by the Cham civilization stand as a reminder of Vietnam's diverse cultural history.

The Allure of Central Vietnamese Cuisine

One cannot visit Central Vietnam without indulging in its unique and flavorful cuisine. Known for its bold and spicy flavors, Central Vietnamese dishes often reflect the influences of royal cuisine, especially in Hue, where the imperial court once demanded intricate, beautifully presented meals. Dishes such as *bun bo Hue* (beef noodle soup), *banh xeo* (crispy pancakes), and *com hen* (rice with baby clams) are just a few examples of the culinary delights awaiting travelers. Hoi An is particularly famous for its *cao lau*, a noodle dish featuring pork, herbs, and crispy rice crackers, as well as its delicate white rose dumplings. Street food is abundant in all the cities, and visitors can easily find affordable and delicious meals at local markets or by the roadside. The food in Central Vietnam is known for its balance of sweet, salty, and spicy flavors, often accompanied by fresh herbs and vegetables, making it a feast for both the palate and the senses.

A Journey Through Time and Tradition

Travelers to Central Vietnam will find themselves on a journey through time, where tradition and modernity coexist harmoniously. In Hue, traditional art forms such as *nha nhac* (royal court music) are still performed, offering visitors a rare chance to experience Vietnam's musical heritage. Meanwhile, in Hoi An, traditional crafts such as lantern-making and silk weaving continue to thrive, with workshops open for visitors who want to learn or simply observe the skilled artisans at work. Festivals play a vital role in the cultural life of Central Vietnam, with many events tied to ancient traditions and local beliefs. The annual Hoi An Lantern Festival, where the town is illuminated by hundreds of colorful lanterns, is a magical experience that transports visitors back to the town's days as a trading hub. In Hue, the biennial Hue Festival celebrates the city's cultural heritage with performances, parades, and exhibitions, turning the ancient city into a vibrant stage for both traditional and modern arts.

Practical Information for Travelers

The best time to visit Central Vietnam is during the dry season, from March to August, when the weather is warm and ideal for beach activities and sightseeing. However, for those who prefer cooler temperatures and fewer crowds, the months of September to February offer a quieter, more serene experience, though travelers should be aware of the rainy season, which can bring occasional typhoons and heavy showers. Accommodation options in Central Vietnam are diverse, catering to all types of travelers, from luxury resorts along the coast to budget-friendly guesthouses in the cities. Hue, Hoi An, and Da Nang all offer a wide range of places to stay, whether you prefer to wake up to the sound of the waves or the charm of an ancient town. Transportation within the region is also convenient, with well-maintained roads and a growing network of buses and trains. Renting a motorbike is a popular option for those who wish to explore at their own pace, especially along the scenic coastal and mountain routes.

6.2 Must-See Attractions

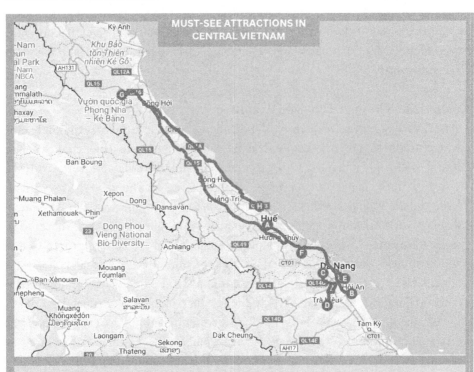

Directions from Hue Imperial City, Lê Huân, Thuận Thành, Huế, Thua Thien Hue, Vietnam to Tam Giang Lagoon, Thua Thien Hue, Vietnam

A
Hue Imperial City, Lê Huân, Thuân Thánh, Huế, Thua Thien Hue, Vietnam

B
Hoi An ancient town, Đường Bạch Đằng, Minh An, Hội An, Quảng Nam, Vietnam

C
Da Nang city, Vietnam

D
My Son Sanctuary, Duy Phú, Duy Xuyên District, Quảng Nam, Vietnam

E
Marble Mountains, Huyền Trân Công Chúa, Hoa Hai, Ngũ Hành Son, Da Nang, Vietnam

F
Bach Ma National Park, Lộc Trì, Phú Lộc, Thua Thien Hue, Vietnam

G
Phong Nha Ke Bang, Phong Natural Heritage Area, Son Trạch, Bô Trạch District, Quang Binh, Vietnam

H
Tarn Giang Lagoon, Thua Thien Hue, Vietnam

6.2.1 Hue Imperial City

Hue Imperial City, located in the heart of central Vietnam, stands as a stunning testament to the country's imperial past. This ancient capital is not only a symbol of Vietnam's rich history but also a cultural treasure that has drawn the interest of historians, travelers, and adventurers alike. A visit to Hue's Imperial City will leave you with a deep understanding of Vietnam's royal heritage and an admiration for its architectural grandeur. This UNESCO World Heritage site is a must-see destination, offering travelers an unforgettable journey into the past.

Where Hue Imperial City is Located
Hue Imperial City is nestled along the banks of the Perfume River in the city of Hue, the former capital of Vietnam. Hue is located in Thua Thien-Hue Province, central Vietnam, about 700 kilometers south of Hanoi and 1,000 kilometers north of Ho Chi Minh City. Its strategic location makes it an accessible stop for travelers exploring the central region of Vietnam, with connections by train, bus, or plane from major cities.

How to Get There
Travelers can reach Hue Imperial City by various means of transportation. The nearest airport is Phu Bai International Airport, located about 15 kilometers from the city center. Flights from Hanoi, Ho Chi Minh City, and Da Nang make

reaching Hue convenient. For those traveling by train, the Reunification Express offers a scenic and comfortable journey through Vietnam's central coast, with Hue being a popular stop on the route. Visitors traveling from Da Nang or Hoi An can take a bus or rent a motorbike for a two-hour scenic drive over the Hai Van Pass, offering breathtaking coastal views. Once in Hue, the Imperial City is easily accessible by taxi, cyclo, or even on foot if you're staying nearby. The city's layout is compact, making it ideal for walking and discovering its historical and cultural wonders.

Entry Fee and Opening Hours
To experience the splendor of Hue Imperial City, visitors are required to pay a modest entry fee. As of 2023, the admission price for adults is approximately 200,000 VND (around $8 USD), with discounts available for students and children. The city opens its gates daily from 7:00 AM to 5:30 PM, giving visitors ample time to explore the vast complex and immerse themselves in its historical depth.

Why Hue Imperial City is Worth Visiting
Hue Imperial City is much more than a collection of ancient buildings. It offers a unique glimpse into Vietnam's imperial past, having served as the political and cultural center of the Nguyen Dynasty from 1802 to 1945. The city was designed following the principles of Feng Shui, with its structures harmoniously arranged to symbolize balance, power, and spiritual protection. The massive complex, surrounded by towering walls and a wide moat, was once home to emperors, their families, and royal officials. Exploring its grounds provides visitors with an intimate look at the opulence and sophistication of the royal court. What makes Hue Imperial City particularly worth visiting is the opportunity to witness Vietnam's ancient architecture, much of which has been meticulously restored after suffering damage during wars. The ornate temples, palaces, gates, and gardens convey a sense of grandeur that is both humbling and awe-inspiring. Whether you're a history enthusiast or simply a curious traveler, the Imperial City will capture your imagination.

Historical and Cultural Significance
The historical significance of Hue Imperial City is profound. It was the seat of power for the Nguyen Dynasty, Vietnam's last ruling family, and remained the country's political capital until the mid-20th century. The complex was built over three decades, beginning in 1804, and was modeled after the Forbidden

City in Beijing. It became the royal residence and served as a religious, educational, and administrative hub for over a century. The Imperial City encompasses numerous historical landmarks, including the Forbidden Purple City (Tu Cam Thanh), which was reserved exclusively for the emperor and his family. During its heyday, the Forbidden City was considered one of the most opulent sections, though much of it was destroyed during the Vietnam War. Restoration efforts have since been undertaken to preserve its historical importance. The citadel also includes other significant structures like the Thai Hoa Palace, where important ceremonies took place, and the Ngo Mon Gate, the main entrance reserved for royal use. The Tombs of the Emperors, located nearby, also provide an intimate view into the legacy of the Nguyen Dynasty. These tombs reflect the deep cultural importance placed on honoring deceased rulers and are equally worth exploring.

What to Do at Hue Imperial City

There is no shortage of things to do within the Imperial City. Visitors can spend hours wandering through the complex's numerous palaces, pavilions, and temples. Don't miss the Noon Gate (Ngo Mon), a striking structure that served as the primary entrance to the Imperial City. Climbing to the top of this gate offers panoramic views of the surrounding grounds and the Perfume River. Exploring Thai Hoa Palace is another highlight. The palace, with its intricately carved wooden pillars and golden throne, was the site of royal meetings and ceremonies. Nearby, the Temple of the Nguyen Dynasty Kings (The Mieu) offers a chance to pay respect to past rulers, whose altars are adorned with offerings and portraits. For those interested in local traditions, the Hue Museum of Royal Antiquities within the complex showcases exquisite artifacts, from royal clothing to elaborate porcelain. Walking through the tranquil royal gardens, you can also experience traditional Vietnamese landscaping that reflects the balance of nature and architecture. A visit to the Imperial City is often complemented by a boat ride along the Perfume River, offering scenic views of the Citadel's walls and the surrounding countryside. The nearby tombs of the Nguyen emperors are also a fascinating extension of the imperial tour, with each tomb reflecting the personality and reign of the ruler it was built for.

Other Information a Visitor Needs to Know

Hue Imperial City can be explored on your own, but hiring a knowledgeable guide is highly recommended to gain deeper insights into its historical and cultural significance. Guides are available at the entrance or through local tour operators. Audio guides are also available in multiple languages for those who prefer a self-guided experience. The best time to visit Hue is from March to May, when the weather is pleasant, with mild temperatures and less rain. If you plan to visit during the summer months (June to August), be prepared for hot and humid conditions, and consider visiting in the morning or late afternoon to avoid the midday heat. Visitors should dress modestly, as this is a historical and culturally important site. Wearing comfortable shoes is essential, as the Imperial City covers a vast area with uneven terrain in some parts. Don't forget to bring water, sunscreen, and a hat for sun protection, especially during the warmer months.

6.2.2 Hoi An Ancient Town

Nestled along the Thu Bon River in Central Vietnam, Hoi An Ancient Town is a living, breathing testament to the country's rich cultural heritage. This charming and historic town, recognized as a UNESCO World Heritage Site, is a treasure trove of preserved architecture, traditional customs, and serene landscapes. As a top destination in Vietnam, Hoi An beckons travelers from around the world with its tranquil beauty, captivating history, and vibrant cultural offerings.

Location and How to Get There

Hoi An Ancient Town is located in Quang Nam Province, about 30 kilometers south of Da Nang. The easiest way to reach Hoi An is by flying into Da Nang International Airport, which offers connections from major cities both domestically and internationally. From Da Nang, you can take a taxi, shuttle, or bus to Hoi An, a journey that typically takes around 45 minutes. For those traveling by train, the Da Nang train station is the nearest rail stop, and from there, similar transportation options are available to reach the town.

Entry Fee and Access

One of the remarkable aspects of visiting Hoi An Ancient Town is its affordability. While there is no general entry fee to explore the town itself, visitors are required to purchase a ticket (around 120,000 VND) to enter certain historical and cultural sites within the town. This ticket gives access to a selection of temples, ancient houses, assembly halls, and museums scattered throughout Hoi An. The funds generated from these tickets contribute to the preservation and maintenance of the town's architectural gems.

Why Hoi An is Worth Visiting

Hoi An is unlike any other destination in Vietnam. Its ancient streets, lined with weathered yellow buildings adorned with lanterns, create an atmosphere of timelessness and tranquility. Walking through Hoi An feels like stepping back in time, as the town's unique blend of Chinese, Japanese, and European influences is reflected in every detail of its architecture. The town is also famous for its peaceful riverside, bustling markets, and vibrant festivals, making it a must-visit for those seeking an immersive cultural experience.

Historical and Cultural Significance

Hoi An's history dates back over 2,000 years, but it rose to prominence as a bustling trading port during the 15th to 19th centuries. Merchants from China, Japan, Portugal, and other countries converged in Hoi An, bringing with them goods, traditions, and architectural styles. This diverse cultural exchange is evident in the town's architecture, with its iconic Japanese Covered Bridge, Chinese Assembly Halls, and European-style colonial buildings. The town also played a significant role in Vietnam's maritime history, serving as a vital link in the spice trade route. Its well-preserved streets and buildings remain a reflection of its golden era, offering a glimpse into the rich multicultural past of the region.

Today, Hoi An continues to celebrate its heritage through traditional craft villages, silk weaving, lantern-making, and local cuisine.

What to Do in Hoi An

Visitors to Hoi An Ancient Town will find an array of activities to immerse themselves in the local culture and history. Begin by strolling through the narrow streets, exploring ancient houses such as the Tan Ky Old House and the Phung Hung Ancient House. These homes, carefully preserved for centuries, offer a window into the lives of the wealthy merchant families who once lived there. The Japanese Covered Bridge, an iconic symbol of Hoi An, is a must-see. This beautifully crafted bridge, adorned with intricate carvings, was built in the 16th century to connect the Japanese and Chinese quarters of the town. Its historical significance and striking design make it one of the most photographed landmarks in the region. For those interested in Hoi An's spiritual side, the Assembly Halls of the Fujian and Cantonese Chinese communities are breathtaking examples of Chinese architecture and religious practices. These vibrant halls are still active centers of worship and cultural celebration, offering visitors the chance to witness local ceremonies. Hoi An's culinary scene is also a highlight of any visit. The town is famous for its regional specialties, including Cao Lau, a unique noodle dish made with local ingredients, and Banh Mi, the beloved Vietnamese sandwich. For a more hands-on experience, visitors can join cooking classes where they learn to prepare these traditional dishes, often beginning with a trip to the bustling central market to source fresh ingredients. In the evenings, the town transforms into a magical display of lanterns. The monthly full moon lantern festival is a spectacle of light, where the streets are illuminated by thousands of glowing lanterns, and traditional music fills the air. Visitors can participate in the festival by releasing their own lanterns into the river, a gesture said to bring good luck and happiness.

Other Information a Visitor Needs to Know

When planning a visit to Hoi An, it's important to consider the weather. The best time to visit is from February to April, when the climate is mild and dry, making it ideal for outdoor exploration. May to August can be quite hot, while the rainy season, from September to January, may bring heavy downpours and the risk of flooding. Hoi An is also an excellent base for exploring the surrounding region. Visitors can take a short trip to the nearby My Son Sanctuary, another UNESCO World Heritage Site, where the ancient ruins of the Cham civilization are set against a backdrop of lush jungle. Alternatively, a visit to the nearby Cua Dai and An Bang beaches offers a chance to unwind by the sea after a day of sightseeing. For those who wish to dive deeper into the local culture, a visit to the traditional craft villages around Hoi An is highly recommended. These villages, such as Thanh Ha Pottery Village and Kim Bong Carpentry Village, have been practicing their crafts for centuries and offer workshops where visitors can try their hand at pottery or wood carving.

Lastly, Hoi An's charm lies not just in its ancient streets but in its welcoming and friendly community. The town is a haven for artists, writers, and those seeking a slower pace of life. The town's unique blend of cultural heritage and modern creativity ensures that every visit is filled with inspiration and discovery.

6.2.3 Da Nang City

Nestled on Vietnam's central coast, Da Nang City is a vibrant and dynamic destination that perfectly blends natural beauty, rich culture, and historical significance. Known for its pristine beaches, majestic mountains, and ancient landmarks, Da Nang offers an unforgettable experience to anyone visiting this rapidly growing city. Whether you're seeking adventure, relaxation, or a deep dive into Vietnam's fascinating heritage, Da Nang has something to offer. It is a must-see for travelers, not only because of its attractions but also for the welcoming atmosphere that makes every visitor feel like a part of its story.

Location and Accessibility

Da Nang is located in central Vietnam, strategically positioned between Hanoi in the north and Ho Chi Minh City in the south. It's a key coastal city with easy access to some of the country's most famous heritage sites, including Hoi An and the ancient capital of Hue. Da Nang International Airport is the major gateway to the city, offering direct flights from major cities around Asia, such as Bangkok, Singapore, Kuala Lumpur, and domestic flights from Hanoi and Ho Chi Minh City. The city is also well connected by train and bus, providing convenient options for overland travel.

Why Da Nang is Worth Visiting

Da Nang stands out as a destination that offers the best of both worlds: modernity and tradition. It is a coastal city blessed with natural beauty, from the golden sands of My Khe Beach to the lush greenery of the Marble Mountains. However, Da Nang is not just about nature; it also boasts a vibrant cultural scene, blending ancient temples with contemporary architecture like the Dragon Bridge. Visitors will find Da Nang the perfect balance of peaceful retreat and bustling city life. The warmth of the locals, delicious food, and world-class hospitality are also reasons why this city is worth visiting.

Historical and Cultural Significance

Da Nang's history dates back over 1,000 years, with its roots in the Champa Kingdom. The Cham people left behind a legacy of temples, statues, and architectural wonders, many of which are preserved in the Cham Museum, one of the most significant cultural institutions in the region. Under French colonial rule, Da Nang became a major port, and it still holds much of that colonial charm in its older neighborhoods. During the Vietnam War, Da Nang was an important airbase for American forces, and remnants of that era can be found scattered throughout the city. This rich history makes Da Nang an exciting place for culture enthusiasts and history buffs alike.

The Majestic Marble Mountains

One of Da Nang's most iconic attractions is the Marble Mountains, a cluster of five limestone and marble hills that rise dramatically from the flat surrounding landscape. Each mountain is named after one of the five elements: metal, wood, water, fire, and earth. Visitors can explore the caves, tunnels, and temples u.. are hidden within these mountains, making it a spiritual and adventurous journey. The panoramic views from the top are breathtaking, offering a sweeping vista of the coastline and cityscape. The Marble Mountains are located around 9 kilometers south of the city center and can be easily accessed by motorbike or taxi. There is a small entry fee, and an additional charge for using the elevator if you prefer to avoid climbing.

The Tranquil My Khe Beach

My Khe Beach is undoubtedly one of Da Nang's crown jewels. Famous for its crystal-clear waters, gentle waves, and soft golden sand, My Khe Beach has earned a place on many lists of the world's best beaches. It stretches for 35 kilometers along the coastline, providing ample space for visitors to find a quiet spot to relax. Whether you're interested in sunbathing, swimming, surfing, or enjoying fresh seafood at one of the beachside restaurants, My Khe Beach is the perfect place to unwind. The beach is free to access and is a short drive from the city center, making it incredibly convenient for visitors.

Ba Na Hills

Perched high in the Truong Son Mountains, Ba Na Hills is a must-see attraction for anyone visiting Da Nang. This French-inspired mountain resort feels like a fairy-tale destination, complete with a replica European village, a massive indoor amusement park, and the iconic Golden Bridge, which appears to be held up by two giant stone hands. The weather here is significantly cooler than in the city, offering a refreshing escape from the heat. The cable car ride to Ba Na Hills is the longest non-stop cable car system in the world, giving visitors a thrilling ride with stunning views. Entry to Ba Na Hills requires a ticket, which includes the cable car ride, and can be purchased online or at the station. The experience is well worth the price for a full day of exploration, relaxation, and incredible photo opportunities.

Son Tra Peninsula

For nature lovers, a visit to the Son Tra Peninsula is an absolute must. This lush, forested peninsula juts out into the sea, offering dramatic cliffs, secluded beaches, and plenty of wildlife, including the endangered red-shanked douc langurs. Son Tra is home to the famous Lady Buddha statue, the tallest of its kind in Vietnam, which stands guard over the Linh Ung Pagoda. The statue is a symbol of peace and protection, and visitors often come here to seek tranquility and breathtaking views over Da Nang's bay. The Son Tra Peninsula is about a 20-minute drive from the city center, and there is no entry fee, making it an ideal spot for a scenic escape.

Dragon Bridge

Da Nang is known for its remarkable bridges, and none is more spectacular than the Dragon Bridge, which spans the Han River in the heart of the city. As its name suggests, this bridge is shaped like a dragon, a symbol of power, prosperity, and good fortune in Vietnamese culture. At night, the bridge is illuminated, and on weekends, it breathes fire and water, creating a truly unforgettable sight. The Dragon Bridge is both a symbol of Da Nang's modernization and a reflection of its cultural heritage, making it a must-visit attraction for anyone exploring the city. Walking across the bridge is free, and it's best viewed from the riverside promenade in the evenings.

What to Do in Da Nang

Beyond its famous landmarks, Da Nang offers a plethora of activities that cater to all types of travelers. Food lovers can indulge in the local cuisine, sampling dishes such as 'mi quang' (a turmeric rice noodle dish), 'banh xeo' (Vietnamese pancakes), and the fresh seafood caught daily. For those interested in shopping, Han Market and Con Market are the places to find everything from traditional handicrafts to local delicacies. Adventurers can explore the Hai Van Pass, a winding mountain road offering some of the best coastal views in Vietnam, or try water sports like jet skiing and paddleboarding along the beaches.

When to Visit Da Nang

Da Nang enjoys a tropical monsoon climate, with the best time to visit being between February and May when the weather is warm and sunny, with little rain. The summer months from June to August are also popular but tend to be hotter. September to January is the rainy season, with occasional typhoons, so it's best to avoid this period if you're planning outdoor activities.

Final Thoughts

Da Nang is a city of contrasts, where old meets new, where nature and modernity coexist in harmony. Its stunning landscapes, rich history, and warm hospitality make it a top destination in central Vietnam. Whether you are drawn to its cultural treasures, the serene beaches, or the promise of adventure in the mountains, Da Nang will captivate your heart. For those seeking an authentic and enriching experience in Vietnam, Da Nang is not to be missed.

6.2.4 My Son Sanctuary

Nestled in the lush heart of central Vietnam, My Son Sanctuary stands as a remarkable testimony to the country's rich cultural and historical tapestry. This UNESCO World Heritage Site is a must-see destination for any traveler drawn to ancient ruins, spirituality, and Vietnam's deeply rooted cultural heritage. More than just a collection of ruins, My Son Sanctuary is a place where history breathes, each structure telling the story of the Champa Kingdom, a civilization that flourished for over a thousand years.

Location and How to Get There
My Son Sanctuary is located approximately 40 kilometers southwest of Hoi An in Quang Nam province, making it a convenient day trip for travelers staying in Hoi An or Da Nang. Surrounded by forested mountains, this hidden gem feels like stepping back into another era, offering tranquility amidst its historical grandeur. Getting to My Son is relatively easy. Visitors can hire a private car, take a motorbike, or join organized tours from either Hoi An or Da Nang. Many opt for guided tours to gain deeper insights into the history of the site. If traveling independently, the drive from Hoi An takes around 1 hour. For those starting in Da Nang, the journey is slightly longer, taking around 1.5 hours. Local buses and tours also run to the sanctuary, offering a more budget-friendly option.

Entry Fee and Opening Hours
As of 2024, the entry fee for My Son Sanctuary is approximately 150,000 VND (around 6-7 USD). This fee includes access to the site and a shuttle bus service that transports visitors from the ticket office to the entrance of the ruins. The sanctuary is open daily from 6:00 AM to 5:00 PM, with early mornings and late afternoons offering cooler temperatures and a more peaceful experience away from larger tour groups.

Why My Son Sanctuary is Worth Visiting
The allure of My Son Sanctuary lies not just in the ancient ruins themselves, but also in the surrounding landscape. Set in a serene valley and framed by green hills, the sanctuary exudes a mystical atmosphere. The peaceful setting, combined with the magnificent architecture, makes My Son a magical

destination for those seeking to delve into Vietnam's ancient past. For history enthusiasts, My Son Sanctuary provides a fascinating glimpse into the Champa civilization, which dates back to the 4th century. Each temple and tower was intricately crafted by Champa artisans, using a unique method of brick masonry that continues to puzzle historians and archaeologists today. Despite suffering significant damage during the Vietnam War, the remaining structures stand as powerful symbols of resilience, reflecting the enduring spirit of the Champa people. The historical significance alone makes My Son worth visiting. It was the religious center of the Champa Kingdom, with temples dedicated to Hindu deities, particularly Shiva, who was regarded as the protector of the kingdom. These ancient temples were where royal ceremonies were held, and they continue to hold spiritual significance for the people of Vietnam today.

Historical and Cultural Significance

My Son Sanctuary holds immense historical and cultural value, not only to Vietnam but to the wider Southeast Asian region. It was once the capital and religious hub of the Champa Kingdom, which thrived from the 4th to the 13th century. This ancient kingdom had strong cultural and trade links with India, as evidenced by the Hindu iconography found throughout the site. The architecture of My Son is heavily influenced by Indian Hinduism, as the Champa people were greatly influenced by Indian traders and scholars. The temples, dedicated to various Hindu deities, exhibit sophisticated craftsmanship in their stone carvings, sculptures, and tower designs. The sanctuary's towers, known as 'kalan', were built to represent the sacred Mount Meru, the center of the universe in Hindu cosmology. These towers served not only as places of worship but also as royal burial chambers. My Son's cultural significance extends beyond its Champa roots. The sanctuary stands as a reminder of Vietnam's tumultuous past, having been heavily bombed during the Vietnam War. Many temples were destroyed, but the remnants stand as poignant symbols of survival and heritage. In 1999, the site was designated as a UNESCO World Heritage Site in recognition of its cultural value and historical significance.

What to Do at My Son Sanctuary

Exploring My Son Sanctuary is an immersive experience. Visitors can wander through the various temple complexes, each offering unique architectural features and a different atmosphere. The temples are spread across a lush valley, surrounded by dense jungle and mountains, creating a sense of seclusion and connection with nature. For those interested in history and architecture, a guided tour is highly recommended. Knowledgeable guides provide fascinating insights into the history of the Champa civilization, the religious significance of the temples, and the mysterious construction techniques that have left researchers in awe. Without such a tour, it can be easy to miss some of the finer details of the site. My Son Sanctuary is also a haven for photographers. The interplay of light, shadow, and the red bricks of the temples creates a striking contrast against the surrounding greenery. Early mornings offer the best lighting for capturing the ethereal beauty of the site. Additionally, traditional Champa dance performances are often held on-site, offering visitors a chance to witness the culture and art of this ancient civilization brought to life.

Additional Information for Visitors

When visiting My Son Sanctuary, it's important to wear comfortable shoes, as much of the site involves walking through uneven terrain and stone pathways. Vietnam's central region can be quite hot, especially during the summer months, so carrying water and sun protection is essential. My Son is best explored in the early morning or late afternoon, not only to avoid the midday heat but also to escape the larger tour groups that tend to arrive mid-morning. The tranquility of the site is best appreciated when there are fewer visitors, allowing you to fully immerse yourself in the atmosphere. Visitors should also take the time to stop by the on-site museum, which houses a small collection of artifacts and provides additional context for the temples. The museum helps to deepen understanding of the site's significance and the Champa culture.

6.3 Hidden Gems of Central Vietnam

Marble Mountains

Tucked away just south of Da Nang, the Marble Mountains rise like ancient sentinels, their limestone peaks crowned with pagodas, caves, and sanctuaries that have drawn pilgrims for centuries. These five marble and limestone hills are named after the five elements—metal, wood, water, fire, and earth—and each carries its own mystical charm. Visitors can explore the many hidden caves within the mountains, where centuries-old Buddhist and Hindu statues reside, illuminated by shafts of natural light that pour through cracks in the rock. Climbing the steep stairs to the summit rewards you with breathtaking panoramic views of the surrounding countryside, stretching all the way to the sparkling coastline. The Marble Mountains offer a serene escape, where the spiritual and the natural come together in perfect harmony. The entry fee is modest, and visitors can hire guides to delve deeper into the rich history and legends of the area.

Bach Ma National Park

Bach Ma National Park, located between Hue and Da Nang, is a hidden gem for nature lovers and adventurers alike. Known for its diverse ecosystems and dramatic landscapes, this national park is home to a wide array of wildlife, including rare species of birds and animals. Visitors to Bach Ma can hike through dense forests, along waterfalls, and up to the park's highest peak, where stunning views of the surrounding mountains and coastline await. The cooler temperatures at higher altitudes provide a welcome relief from the heat of the lowlands, making it an ideal destination for trekking and nature walks. Bach Ma National Park also offers camping facilities and eco-lodges, allowing visitors to fully immerse themselves in the natural beauty of the region. Entry to the park is reasonably priced, and guided tours are available for those who want to learn more about the flora and fauna that call this park home.

Phong Nha-Ke Bang

Hidden beneath the dense jungles of Quang Binh Province, Phong Nha-Ke Bang National Park is home to some of the world's most impressive caves, including the renowned Son Doong Cave—the largest cave on the planet. For those who seek adventure, Phong Nha offers a chance to explore these breathtaking underground worlds, filled with towering stalagmites, underground rivers, and immense caverns. The park is also a UNESCO World Heritage Site, recognized for its incredible biodiversity and geological significance. Visitors can take boat trips into Phong Nha Cave, trek through the jungle to reach the stunning Paradise Cave, or embark on multi-day expeditions into Son Doong for the ultimate adventure. The park is also home to pristine rivers, towering limestone peaks, and an abundance of wildlife, making it a paradise for nature lovers. Entry fees and tour prices vary depending on the cave you wish to explore, but the experience is truly unforgettable.

Tam Giang Lagoon

Just outside of Hue, the serene waters of Tam Giang Lagoon stretch out toward the horizon, creating a peaceful escape from the bustling cities. This vast lagoon is the largest in Southeast Asia, and it is still largely untouched by mass tourism. Fishermen glide across the water in their traditional boats, casting nets in the golden light of dawn or dusk, while water buffalo graze along the shore. For visitors seeking a more authentic experience of rural Vietnam, a trip to Tam Giang offers a unique opportunity to immerse oneself in the rhythms of local life. The lagoon is also a haven for birdwatchers, as it attracts a variety of migratory birds throughout the year. Visitors can take boat tours to explore the lagoon, visit local fishing villages, and even enjoy a fresh seafood meal at one of the simple, family-run restaurants along the shore. Entry to the lagoon is free, and tours can be arranged with local guides who know the area intimately.

6.4 Beaches and Water Activities

Vietnam's coastline stretches for over 3,000 kilometers, offering an array of stunning beaches and vibrant water activities that invite visitors to immerse themselves in the country's natural beauty. From the clear waters of tropical islands to the lively coastal cities, the beaches of Vietnam cater to all kinds of travelers, whether they're seeking relaxation or adventure. Water sports such as snorkeling, kayaking, and surfing are readily available, adding excitement to any beach visit. Below are five exceptional destinations that offer unforgettable water experiences and showcase Vietnam's coastal charm.

Nha Trang

Nha Trang, often regarded as the beach capital of Vietnam, is known for its crystal-clear waters and vibrant marine life. The city's main beach, Tran Phu Beach, is the heart of activity, where visitors can indulge in a variety of water sports such as jet skiing, parasailing, and snorkeling. For those looking to explore beneath the waves, Hon Mun Island, just a boat ride away, offers excellent diving and snorkeling spots with rich coral reefs. Nha Trang is located in southern Vietnam, easily accessible by plane, with Cam Ranh International Airport just 30 kilometers away. Taxi fares from the airport to the city center are around $12 to $15. Entry to the beach is free, but the cost of renting equipment for water sports ranges from $10 to $50, depending on the activity. Nha Trang's blend of lively city vibes and beach adventures makes it a must-visit destination for water enthusiasts.

Phu Quoc

Phu Quoc, Vietnam's largest island, is a paradise for beach lovers and water sport enthusiasts alike. Located off the southwestern coast of Vietnam, Phu Quoc is known for its white sandy beaches and clear, turquoise waters. Long Beach, the island's most famous stretch of sand, is perfect for sunbathing, swimming, and kayaking, while more secluded beaches like Bai Sao offer a quieter escape. For those interested in snorkeling, the An Thoi Archipelago, a group of small islands just off Phu Quoc's southern tip, provides some of the best underwater scenery in Vietnam. Flights from Ho Chi Minh City to Phu Quoc take about an hour, with prices ranging from $30 to $100 depending on the season. Once on the island, taxis or motorbike rentals are popular means of transportation, with taxi fares from the airport to Long Beach costing around $10. Beach access is generally free, and the price for a day of snorkeling or diving ranges from $20 to $50, depending on the tour. Phu Quoc's serene atmosphere and rich marine biodiversity make it a perfect destination for those seeking both relaxation and adventure.

Da Nang

Da Nang, located along Vietnam's central coast, is home to some of the most beautiful beaches in the country, including My Khe Beach and Non Nuoc Beach. My Khe Beach, often referred to as "China Beach," is popular for surfing, especially between September and March when the waves are ideal. For those looking for a more relaxed experience, Non Nuoc Beach offers calm waters perfect for swimming and paddleboarding. Da Nang is easily accessible by air, with Da Nang International Airport just 6 kilometers from the city center. A taxi from the airport to the beach costs around $7 to $10. Beach access is free, but renting surfing equipment or booking lessons costs approximately $20 to $40 for a half-day session. With its blend of vibrant city life and stunning coastline, Da Nang is a top destination for visitors seeking both water sports and a dynamic cultural scene.

Mui Ne

Mui Ne, a coastal town known for its strong winds and long sandy beaches, is the perfect destination for windsurfing and kitesurfing enthusiasts. The consistent winds from November to April make Mui Ne one of the best spots in Southeast Asia for these sports. The town's main beach, stretching for miles, offers ideal conditions for both beginners and advanced surfers. For those less inclined toward extreme sports, the calm waters of the morning are perfect for swimming and stand-up paddleboarding. Mui Ne is located about 220 kilometers northeast of Ho Chi Minh City, and visitors can reach it by train or bus. A bus ride from Ho Chi Minh City to Mui Ne costs around $10 and takes about 5 hours. Beach access is free, but equipment rentals for kitesurfing and windsurfing range from $30 to $50 per hour. Mui Ne's reputation as Vietnam's

101

windsurfing and kitesurfing haven ensures it remains a favorite among thrill-seekers.

Con Dao Islands

The Con Dao Islands, a remote archipelago off the southern coast of Vietnam, offer some of the most pristine diving and snorkeling spots in the country. The islands are surrounded by crystal-clear waters that boast a rich variety of marine life, including vibrant coral reefs, sea turtles, and even dugongs. Con Son, the main island, is home to several diving schools where visitors can book guided diving tours. Dam Trau Beach, with its powdery white sand and turquoise waters, is a favorite spot for both diving and sunbathing. To get to the Con Dao Islands, visitors can take a one-hour flight from Ho Chi Minh City, with ticket prices ranging from $100 to $150. Once on the islands, motorbikes are the best way to get around, with rentals costing around $7 per day. The cost of diving tours ranges from $50 to $100 depending on the depth and duration of the dive. The untouched beauty of the Con Dao Islands makes them a must-visit destination for nature lovers and underwater explorers.

CHAPTER 7
DISCOVERING SOUTHERN VIETNAM

7.1 Overview of Southern Vietnam

Southern Vietnam is a region that blends vibrant cities, tranquil countryside, and a rich tapestry of history and culture. It is a destination where the energy of urban life seamlessly coexists with the slow-paced rhythm of rural communities. As the heart of the Mekong Delta, this region thrives on its waterways, lush landscapes, and a cultural vibrancy that makes it one of Vietnam's most dynamic areas. Southern Vietnam is an essential part of any travel itinerary, offering both adventure and relaxation to the curious traveler. Whether you are drawn to the bustling streets of Ho Chi Minh City or the peaceful backwaters of the Mekong, this region will captivate you with its charm and diversity.

Cultural and Historical Significance

The culture of southern Vietnam is deeply rooted in its history, influenced by centuries of colonialism, war, and the resilience of its people. From ancient Cham ruins to the remnants of the Vietnam War, the region is filled with landmarks that tell stories of conflict, survival, and the blending of different cultures. French colonial architecture stands proudly in the heart of cities like Ho Chi Minh City, alongside Buddhist pagodas and Catholic churches, reflecting the cultural intersections that shape the area. Southern Vietnam's history is rich and complex, but it is its people—warm, welcoming, and eager to share their stories—that make the experience of visiting so unforgettable.

The Mekong Delta

At the heart of southern Vietnam lies the Mekong Delta, a vast maze of rivers, swamps, and islands that serves as the lifeblood of the region. Known as Vietnam's "rice bowl," the delta is a fertile area where agriculture thrives, producing rice, tropical fruits, and seafood. For visitors, the Mekong offers a unique glimpse into traditional Vietnamese life. A boat trip through the delta's narrow waterways reveals floating markets, where vendors sell goods directly from their boats, and small villages where life has remained largely unchanged for generations. The Mekong Delta is a serene escape from the bustling cities, allowing visitors to immerse themselves in the natural beauty and rural charm of the region.

Ho Chi Minh City

No trip to southern Vietnam is complete without visiting Ho Chi Minh City, the region's largest metropolis and economic powerhouse. Formerly known as Saigon, the city is a whirlwind of activity, with motorbikes whizzing through the streets, towering skyscrapers, and markets buzzing with energy. Yet beneath its modern exterior, Ho Chi Minh City is a place rich in history, with landmarks like the Reunification Palace and the War Remnants Museum offering a window into the country's past. The city's food scene is also legendary, from high-end restaurants to street vendors serving dishes that showcase the best of Vietnamese cuisine. For those seeking a vibrant and exciting urban experience, Ho Chi Minh City is an essential stop.

Beaches and Coastal Retreats

Southern Vietnam is also home to some of the country's most stunning beaches, offering a peaceful contrast to the energetic cities. Along the coastline, destinations like Vung Tau, Phu Quoc, and the Con Dao Islands provide idyllic beach retreats for travelers seeking relaxation. Vung Tau is a popular getaway for those living in Ho Chi Minh City, offering a mix of beachfront resorts and local seafood restaurants. Phu Quoc, an island paradise in the Gulf of Thailand, is known for its white sandy beaches, crystal-clear waters, and lush rainforests. It's the perfect destination for travelers looking to unwind in a tropical setting, with plenty of opportunities for snorkeling, diving, and exploring the island's natural beauty.

Local Life and Traditions

Southern Vietnam is a place where traditions hold strong, even as the region rapidly modernizes. Visitors to the rural areas of the Mekong Delta will witness a way of life that has remained largely unchanged for centuries. Farmers tend to their rice paddies, fishermen cast their nets in the rivers, and families gather around small wooden houses built on stilts to share meals. Festivals and religious ceremonies are also integral to life in southern Vietnam, from the bustling Tet celebrations that mark the Lunar New Year to the colorful Nghinh Ong Festival, which honors the whale, a revered animal in Vietnamese culture. Experiencing these traditions firsthand offers visitors a deeper understanding of the cultural richness of the region.

Getting Around Southern Vietnam

Traveling around southern Vietnam is relatively easy, with a variety of transportation options available to visitors. In cities like Ho Chi Minh, buses and taxis are readily available, while many tourists opt to rent motorbikes for a more immersive experience. For those looking to explore the Mekong Delta, boat trips and ferry services provide a scenic way to navigate the region's waterways. Domestic flights and buses also connect major destinations, making it convenient to travel between the beaches, cities, and rural areas of southern Vietnam. The region's well-developed infrastructure ensures that visitors can easily explore its many attractions, whether they're seeking the excitement of urban life or the tranquility of the countryside.

A Region of Contrasts and Diversity

What makes southern Vietnam truly special is the diversity it offers. It's a region where the ancient coexists with the modern, where the urban meets the rural, and where nature's beauty contrasts with human ingenuity. From the neon-lit streets of Ho Chi Minh City to the quiet rice fields of the Mekong, southern Vietnam is a land of contrasts that invites exploration. It's a place where each day brings a new discovery, whether it's the flavors of a street food stall, the serenity of a floating village, or the awe-inspiring history that lives in its architecture and monuments.

7.2 Must-See Attractions

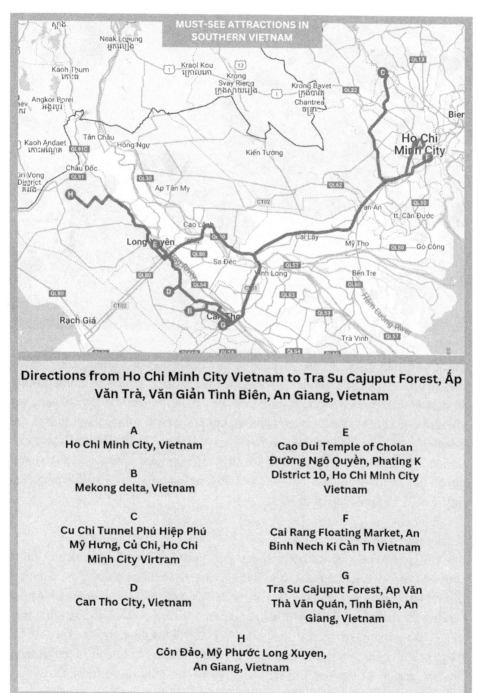

Directions from Ho Chi Minh City Vietnam to Tra Su Cajuput Forest, Ấp Văn Trà, Văn Giản Tỉnh Biên, An Giang, Vietnam

A
Ho Chi Minh City, Vietnam

B
Mekong delta, Vietnam

C
Cu Chi Tunnel Phú Hiệp Phú Mỹ Hưng, Củ Chi, Ho Chi Minh City Virtram

D
Can Tho City, Vietnam

E
Cao Dui Temple of Cholan Đường Ngô Quyền, Phating K District 10, Ho Chi Minh City Vietnam

F
Cai Rang Floating Market, An Binh Nech Ki Cần Th Vietnam

G
Tra Su Cajuput Forest, Ap Văn Thà Văn Quán, Tình Biên, An Giang, Vietnam

H
Côn Đảo, Mỹ Phước Long Xuyen, An Giang, Vietnam

106

7.2.1 Ho Chi Minh City

Ho Chi Minh City, formerly known as Saigon, is a vibrant and bustling metropolis that stands as one of Vietnam's most essential destinations. Located in the southern region of the country, this city blends historical significance with the fast-paced energy of modern life, creating a unique atmosphere that is both charming and chaotic. As the largest city in Vietnam, Ho Chi Minh City offers a variety of experiences, from its rich history and cultural heritage to its dynamic street life and world-class cuisine. For anyone planning to visit Vietnam, this city should be at the top of the list.

A Dynamic Location
Ho Chi Minh City is situated along the banks of the Saigon River in the southern part of Vietnam, about 1,700 kilometers south of Hanoi, the country's capital. It is easily accessible by air, with Tan Son Nhat International Airport serving as the main gateway for international visitors. From the airport, it's a quick 30-minute drive to the city center, depending on traffic. Public transportation options like buses and taxis are readily available, though many tourists prefer to explore the city on foot or by renting motorbikes to fully immerse themselves in the local way of life.

The Rich Cultural and Historical Significance

The history of Ho Chi Minh City is rich and complex, marked by its pivotal role during the French colonial era and the Vietnam War. Originally a small fishing village, the city grew rapidly during the 19th century under French rule, becoming the cultural and economic center of southern Vietnam. Today, its colonial architecture, historic landmarks, and war remnants tell the story of a city that has endured and evolved. Visiting sites like the War Remnants Museum or Reunification Palace provides a sobering insight into the city's turbulent past, while walking through its colonial districts offers a glimpse into its layered history.

Why Ho Chi Minh City is Worth Visiting

Ho Chi Minh City is more than just a historical site; it's a living, breathing entity where tradition meets modernity. The energy of the city is palpable. Bustling streets filled with motorbikes, colorful markets, and food vendors create a sensory overload that is both overwhelming and invigorating. The city is a hub for art, music, and fashion, and it's impossible not to feel its creative pulse. Whether you are exploring ancient pagodas, sipping coffee in a French-style café, or diving into a bowl of steaming pho, the city promises unforgettable moments at every corner. Beyond its history, the city's culinary scene is one of the most vibrant in Southeast Asia. From high-end dining to street food stalls, the flavors of Vietnam are on full display here. A visitor should not leave without trying dishes like banh mi, pho, or the local specialty, com tam (broken rice). The Ben Thanh Market, one of the city's oldest and most famous markets, is the perfect place to explore the culinary delights of the city while also shopping for local crafts, textiles, and souvenirs.

Things to Do in Ho Chi Minh City

There is no shortage of activities to fill your days in Ho Chi Minh City. Start by visiting some of its most famous landmarks, such as the Notre-Dame Cathedral Basilica of Saigon and the Central Post Office, both stunning examples of French colonial architecture. For those interested in Vietnam's history, a visit to the War Remnants Museum is a must. It offers a sobering look at the Vietnam War from the Vietnamese perspective, with exhibits that include wartime photographs, military equipment, and powerful stories of resilience. The Reunification Palace, also known as Independence Palace, is another key historical site. It was here that the Vietnam War officially ended in 1975 when a North Vietnamese tank crashed through its gates. Today, the palace remains almost exactly as it was, and visitors can explore its various rooms, halls, and underground bunkers, giving them a glimpse into the city's political past. For a more relaxing experience, take a boat tour along the Saigon River, where you can see the city from a different perspective. Alternatively, visit one of the many parks and green spaces that dot the city, such as Tao Dan Park, a peaceful oasis in the midst of the urban jungle. At night, the city comes alive with vibrant nightlife, from rooftop bars with panoramic views to local beer halls where you can share a drink with locals and travelers alike.

How to Get There and Entry Fees
Getting around Ho Chi Minh City is relatively easy, thanks to its extensive network of taxis, buses, and motorbike rentals. Taxis are inexpensive, though it's important to ensure the meter is running to avoid overpaying. Many visitors also use ride-hailing apps like Grab to get around, offering a convenient and reliable way to travel across the city. For those who prefer a more adventurous option, renting a motorbike is a popular way to explore the city, but be prepared for chaotic traffic and be cautious if you are not an experienced rider.

Most of the city's attractions, including the War Remnants Museum and Reunification Palace, charge a modest entry fee of about 40,000 to 60,000 VND (approximately $2 to $3 USD). These fees are affordable, making it easy to visit multiple sites during your stay.

Final Thoughts for Visitors
Ho Chi Minh City is a destination that offers a fascinating mix of history, culture, and modernity. It is a city where you can lose yourself in its chaotic streets, yet find peace in its historic sites and natural spaces. For those looking to understand Vietnam's past while embracing its vibrant present, Ho Chi Minh City is an essential stop. Whether you are a history buff, a foodie, or simply a curious traveler, this city has something to offer everyone. With its rich blend of old and new, Ho Chi Minh City is more than just a stopover on your way to other parts of Vietnam—it's a place where memories are made and stories are lived. The city invites you to explore, to learn, and to be a part of its ongoing narrative, one that continues to evolve with each passing day. If you're seeking an authentic and immersive travel experience, Ho Chi Minh City should be at the top of your list.

7.2.2 Mekong Delta

The Mekong Delta is one of the most captivating and essential destinations for any traveler venturing to southern Vietnam. Known as the "Rice Bowl" of the country, the Delta is a vibrant region of intricate waterways, lush green landscapes, and rich cultural traditions. Its endless rice paddies, floating markets, and charming villages create an unforgettable backdrop for those seeking an authentic and immersive experience. Beyond its natural beauty, the Mekong Delta holds deep historical and cultural significance, making it a must-visit for those eager to understand the soul of Vietnam.

Location and How to Get There
Located in the southwestern region of Vietnam, the Mekong Delta spans over 15,000 square miles and consists of a network of rivers, swamps, and islands. It begins south of Ho Chi Minh City and stretches all the way to the Gulf of Thailand. The region is accessible by car or bus from Ho Chi Minh City, with most trips taking about 2 to 4 hours, depending on your destination within the Delta. You can also opt for guided tours that often include boat trips along the river, offering a seamless way to explore the waterways. Travelers looking for a more independent adventure can rent a scooter or take public transportation to key towns such as Can Tho, My Tho, or Ben Tre, which serve as excellent starting points for exploring the Delta.

Entry Fee and Accessibility

There is no general entry fee to the Mekong Delta, but specific activities or attractions may have small charges, such as boat tours or entry into nature reserves. Most floating markets and villages are free to visit, though hiring a local guide or booking boat services might cost around $5 to $20, depending on the length and type of tour. For travelers on a budget, the region offers plenty of affordable accommodations and dining options, making it accessible to a wide range of visitors.

Why the Mekong Delta is Worth Visiting

What makes the Mekong Delta truly special is its unique combination of natural beauty and vibrant local life. The region's charm lies in its floating villages, bustling markets, and serene countryside, where daily life revolves around the rivers and canals. The slow pace of life here offers a stark contrast to the hustle of Ho Chi Minh City, making it an ideal escape for those looking to unwind and experience the traditional Vietnamese way of life. Whether it's gliding through narrow canals shaded by coconut trees or watching the sunrise over vast rice fields, the Mekong Delta delivers an atmosphere of tranquility and timelessness that is rare to find.

Historical and Cultural Significance

The Mekong Delta is not only important as an agricultural hub but also holds great historical and cultural significance for Vietnam. For centuries, the Delta has been the lifeline of the southern Vietnamese population, providing sustenance and shaping the way of life. During the Vietnam War, the Delta was a key battleground, and remnants of this period, such as tunnels and memorials, can still be found in the area. The local population is a diverse mix of ethnic groups, including the Khmer, Vietnamese, and Chinese communities, each contributing to the region's distinct cultural flavor. Traditional music, like the "Đờn ca tài tử" folk songs, which originated here, is now recognized by UNESCO as an Intangible Cultural Heritage, adding further cultural depth to your visit.

Activities and What to Do in the Mekong Delta

One of the highlights of any visit to the Mekong Delta is experiencing the iconic floating markets, where locals buy and sell everything from fruits and vegetables to handmade crafts, directly from their boats. The Can Tho Floating Market, in particular, is one of the most famous, offering visitors the chance to immerse themselves in the bustling atmosphere of trade on water. A boat ride at dawn through these markets allows travelers to witness the authentic exchange of goods and local life at its finest.

Exploring the various canals and smaller waterways is another must-do activity. Boat tours take visitors through serene, narrow channels, lined with coconut groves and stilted houses. These trips often include stops at local villages where travelers can interact with the friendly locals, learn about traditional crafts, and sample regional delicacies such as coconut candy, fresh fruit, and fish. For nature lovers, the Delta is also home to several bird sanctuaries and national parks, such as Tra Su Cajuput Forest. Here, visitors can enjoy bird-watching, take eco-friendly boat trips through flooded forests, and experience the rich biodiversity of the area. The Delta's wetland ecosystems are a haven for wildlife, including rare bird species, making it a great destination for photographers and nature enthusiasts alike.

Additional Information for Visitors
The best time to visit the Mekong Delta is during the dry season, which runs from November to April, as this period offers pleasant weather and clear skies, perfect for outdoor activities. The rainy season, from May to October, can be challenging for travel, as roads may become flooded, though the region's lush landscapes during this time have their own appeal. If you're visiting the Delta, consider staying in a homestay for a truly authentic experience. Many local families open their homes to visitors, providing a unique opportunity to live like a local, enjoying home-cooked meals and learning about the day-to-day life of the Mekong people. This not only supports the local economy but also allows you to form a deeper connection with the region.

7.2.3 Cu Chi Tunnels

In southern Vietnam, just a short drive from the bustling city of Ho Chi Minh, lies one of the most captivating and historically significant attractions in the country: the Cu Chi Tunnels. For any traveler interested in history, culture, or the indomitable spirit of human resilience, the Cu Chi Tunnels offer a profound experience that brings the stories of Vietnam's past vividly to life. Far more than just an underground maze, the tunnels serve as a reminder of the struggles faced by the Vietnamese people during the Vietnam War, and they provide a powerful insight into the ingenuity, determination, and survival of those who lived through it.

Location and How to Get There

The Cu Chi Tunnels are located approximately 70 kilometers northwest of Ho Chi Minh City. For visitors coming from the city, getting to the site is relatively easy and can be done through several means of transportation. Most travelers opt to join a guided tour, which often includes round-trip transportation from Ho Chi Minh City. These tours typically take a half-day, leaving in the morning and returning by the afternoon. Alternatively, those seeking a more independent trip can hire a private car, motorbike, or take public buses that run regularly to Cu Chi. The journey typically takes around one and a half to two hours, depending on traffic.

Entry Fees and Practical Information

Entry to the Cu Chi Tunnels is reasonably priced, making it accessible to a wide range of travelers. As of the most recent updates, the entry fee is around VND 90,000, with additional costs if you choose to join a guided tour or experience other on-site attractions such as firing live rounds at the nearby shooting range. The tunnels are open daily from early morning until late afternoon, offering ample time for exploration. It's advisable to wear comfortable clothing and shoes, as the site involves walking, crouching, and navigating through narrow spaces, giving you a small taste of the challenging conditions faced by those who lived in the tunnels.

The Historical and Cultural Significance of the Tunnels

The Cu Chi Tunnels were constructed during the Vietnam War as a strategic network of underground passages used by the Viet Cong to evade American forces. These tunnels, which stretched over 250 kilometers at their peak, served as hiding spots, supply routes, living quarters, and hospitals for the soldiers. The tunnel system was ingeniously designed, with multiple levels, hidden entrances, and ventilation shafts that allowed the Viet Cong to move undetected. Life inside the tunnels was far from easy; the soldiers endured extreme heat, poor ventilation, and the constant threat of discovery. However, the tunnels played a critical role in the eventual victory of the North Vietnamese forces. Today, the Cu Chi Tunnels stand as a testament to the resilience and resourcefulness of the Vietnamese people. They are more than just a historical monument; they are a symbol of the human will to survive against all odds. Visitors who explore the tunnels come away with a deep sense of respect for the sacrifices made during the war and an appreciation for the cultural heritage that shaped modern Vietnam.

What to Do and See at Cu Chi

Exploring the Cu Chi Tunnels is a fascinating and immersive experience. Upon arrival, visitors are typically introduced to the site through a short documentary that provides historical context and sets the stage for the tour. From there, you are guided through sections of the tunnels, where you can physically enter and crawl through the tight, dimly lit passages. While the tunnels have been slightly widened to accommodate modern tourists, they still give a sense of the claustrophobic conditions endured by those who lived there.

In addition to exploring the tunnels themselves, there are several other points of interest at the site. You can observe booby traps and various weapons used during the war, as well as see reconstructed bunkers, command centers, and kitchens that demonstrate how life was sustained underground. For those interested in a more interactive experience, there is a shooting range on-site where visitors can try their hand at firing a variety of historical firearms, including AK-47s and M16 rifles, for an additional fee. There is also a poignant aspect to visiting Cu Chi. As you move through the site, you are constantly reminded of the human stories behind the war. The tunnels are not just relics of the past but echoes of the lives that were lived, fought, and lost in this harsh landscape. The memorials and exhibits honor the courage and determination of those who called the tunnels home, offering visitors an opportunity to reflect on the cost of war and the strength of the human spirit.

Why It's Worth Visiting

A visit to the Cu Chi Tunnels is an unforgettable experience that brings history to life in a way few other sites can. Whether you are a history buff, a cultural enthusiast, or simply someone with a curiosity about the past, the tunnels offer something unique and profound. Walking through these underground corridors, crouching in the same spaces where soldiers once hid, and seeing the remnants of a war that shaped a nation creates a deeply personal connection to the history of Vietnam. More than just a museum, the Cu Chi Tunnels allow you to physically engage with history. It is one thing to read about the war in books or see it on a screen, but it is something else entirely to feel the oppressive heat of the tunnels, to imagine living in such conditions, and to understand the strategies and sacrifices that were necessary for survival. The experience leaves visitors with a deep respect for the resilience of the Vietnamese people and a greater understanding of the complexities of the Vietnam War.

7.2.4 Can Tho City

Can Tho City is one of Vietnam's hidden gems, nestled in the heart of the lush Mekong Delta. Known for its rich history, vibrant culture, and breathtaking natural landscapes, Can Tho is a destination that enchants travelers with its laid-back charm and unique experiences. The city is often referred to as the "rice basket" of Vietnam, and its deep connection to the Mekong River makes it an essential stop for anyone looking to understand the soul of southern Vietnam.

Location and How to Get There
Located about 170 kilometers southwest of Ho Chi Minh City, Can Tho is easily accessible by bus or car. The journey typically takes around three and a half hours, making it a perfect escape from the hustle and bustle of the city. You can find buses departing from Ho Chi Minh City's Mien Tay Bus Station, or alternatively, private car rentals are available for a more comfortable journey. Can Tho also has its own small airport, Can Tho International Airport, which offers flights from major Vietnamese cities, including Hanoi and Da Nang, making it even more accessible for domestic and international travelers.

No Entry Fee but Priceless Experiences

Unlike many tourist attractions that require an entry fee, Can Tho City itself is an open and welcoming destination, offering its beauty freely to all who visit. Most of the attractions within the city, such as its iconic floating markets and riverside promenades, are accessible without any specific charges. However, guided boat tours or other organized activities, such as visits to the fruit orchards or eco-tourism areas, may come with small fees. Regardless, the value of what you experience here is immeasurable. The opportunity to immerse yourself in local life along the Mekong River is one that money can't buy.

Why It's Worth Visiting

Can Tho is a city where tradition meets modernity. Its historical significance dates back to its days as a trading hub in the Mekong Delta, and it continues to thrive as a key agricultural and economic center in Vietnam. The floating markets of Can Tho, especially the famous Cai Rang Floating Market, are a testament to this history. Here, boats brimming with fresh fruits, vegetables, and local produce bob on the river at dawn, creating a colorful and lively scene. This unique way of life, which revolves around the water, allows visitors to witness the deep-rooted connection between the people of Can Tho and the Mekong River. Culturally, Can Tho is a blend of Vietnamese, Khmer, and Chinese influences. This diversity is reflected in the city's architecture, food, and festivals. The Ong Temple, located along the riverfront, is a fine example of Chinese architecture and serves as a place of worship for the city's Chinese-Vietnamese community. The Binh Thuy Ancient House, another must-see, offers insight into the life of a wealthy landowner during French colonial times. Visiting these sites gives travelers a deeper understanding of Can Tho's rich cultural and historical layers.

What to Do in Can Tho

Can Tho offers a range of activities that cater to every type of traveler. One of the highlights is undoubtedly the Cai Rang Floating Market, where visitors can take an early morning boat ride to experience the lively trade on the water. Watching local vendors sell everything from exotic fruits to freshly cooked meals from their boats is an unforgettable experience. For those interested in food, Can Tho's floating market is also an opportunity to taste the freshest tropical produce available. Another must-see is the Binh Thuy Ancient House, a beautiful colonial-era home that is famous for its well-preserved architecture and peaceful gardens. A visit here feels like stepping back in time, offering a

116

glimpse into the opulent lifestyle of the past. Nature lovers can explore Can Tho's lush fruit orchards and ecological areas, where you can take leisurely bike rides or strolls through peaceful, green landscapes. Phong Dien and My Khanh are two popular eco-tourism sites where visitors can pick their own fruit, enjoy traditional music performances, and sample local delicacies. For those looking to relax, Can Tho's riverside promenade is perfect for an evening stroll. Watching the sunset over the Mekong River while sipping a coconut drink or enjoying some street food from the local vendors is a magical way to end the day. The riverfront is also home to numerous cafes, restaurants, and bars, where you can sit back and take in the bustling atmosphere of the city.

Historical and Cultural Significance

The Mekong River has always been central to life in Can Tho, shaping its history and culture. The floating markets that define the city's charm are not just tourist attractions but a vital part of the region's economy and way of life. Can Tho's position as a trading hub in the Delta has allowed it to thrive for centuries, and today it remains an important link in Vietnam's agricultural production, especially in rice and fruit cultivation. Visitors who want to understand the agricultural roots of Vietnam should look no further than Can Tho, where modern farming techniques blend with age-old traditions. Culturally, Can Tho reflects the rich diversity of southern Vietnam. Its temples, festivals, and cuisine offer a mosaic of influences, from Khmer and Chinese to indigenous Vietnamese. This cultural diversity makes Can Tho a fascinating destination for anyone interested in exploring the multi-ethnic fabric of the region. Visiting Can Tho is an opportunity to step into a world where ancient traditions are still alive and thriving amidst the demands of the modern world.

Why Can Tho is a Must-See

In conclusion, Can Tho City stands out as a must-see destination in southern Vietnam, not only for its floating markets and riverside charm but also for its deep cultural and historical roots. It offers a unique combination of natural beauty, cultural richness, and historical significance that makes it unlike anywhere else in the world. Whether you're interested in sampling exotic fruits at the floating market, wandering through colonial-era architecture, or simply soaking in the peaceful atmosphere along the Mekong River, Can Tho has something for everyone. For any traveler seeking an authentic and immersive experience, Can Tho is the perfect gateway to the Mekong Delta and beyond. Its vibrant markets, beautiful landscapes, and welcoming people offer a warm and enriching introduction to the heart of Vietnam.

7.3 Hidden Gems of Southern Vietnam

Southern Vietnam, often overshadowed by the buzzing streets of Ho Chi Minh City and the iconic Mekong Delta, holds a treasure trove of hidden gems. Tucked away from the well-trodden tourist paths are serene landscapes, cultural treasures, and local experiences that paint a deeper, more intimate picture of Vietnam's southern region.

Con Dao Islands

Off the southern coast of Vietnam lies the breathtaking Con Dao Islands, an archipelago that remains largely untouched by mass tourism. Known for its pristine beaches, lush forests, and crystal-clear waters, this island destination offers a peaceful escape for those looking to immerse themselves in nature. The islands are steeped in history, once serving as a prison during the French colonial period, and now housing memorials that honor Vietnam's turbulent past. Visitors can explore these historic sites while also enjoying the serene beauty of the beaches, where snorkeling, diving, and turtle-watching opportunities abound. Con Dao's isolation makes it a perfect spot for those seeking tranquility and reflection amidst unspoiled natural beauty.

Cao Dai Temple

Nestled in the town of Tay Ninh, a few hours from Ho Chi Minh City, is the spectacular Cao Dai Temple, a vibrant and colorful place of worship that represents the heart of Cao Dai, a unique Vietnamese religion. The temple, with its intricate mosaics and striking colors, is a visual feast that fuses elements of Eastern and Western religions, incorporating Buddhism, Taoism, Confucianism, and even Catholicism. Visiting the Cao Dai Temple allows one to witness the noon prayer ceremony, an unforgettable experience that offers a glimpse into the spiritual practices of the Cao Dai followers. This hidden gem is not only a cultural and religious experience but also a reflection of Vietnam's rich spiritual diversity.

The Floating Markets of Can Tho

The floating markets of Can Tho are an authentic slice of life on the Mekong Delta that few outside travelers take the time to fully appreciate. Visiting these early-morning markets is a vibrant, sensory experience where locals trade goods from boats, offering a colorful array of fruits, vegetables, and traditional Vietnamese fare. Cai Rang, the largest floating market, provides visitors with a glimpse into the daily rhythms of the Mekong River. The experience is both lively and intimate, with traders calling out their offerings and visitors being able to sample the fresh produce right from the boats. The best time to visit is at dawn, when the markets are in full swing, allowing travelers to savor both the unique culture of the region and the serenity of the Mekong as it wakes with the sun.

Mui Ne's Red and White Sand Dunes

The coastal town of Mui Ne, known for its beautiful beaches and relaxed atmosphere, holds a lesser-known surprise – the towering red and white sand dunes that rise dramatically from the coastal landscape. These dunes, stretching across vast expanses, resemble a desert within Vietnam and provide an unexpected backdrop to the lush, tropical surroundings. The white dunes, especially, offer visitors a chance to try sandboarding or take a jeep tour to explore the area. As the sun sets, the sands take on a golden hue, making it a perfect spot for photographers and those seeking solitude in a surreal environment. Mui Ne's dunes are a hidden gem for those looking for adventure combined with breathtaking natural beauty.

Tra Su Mangrove Forest

Located in the An Giang Province near the Cambodian border, Tra Su Mangrove Forest is a serene, almost mystical destination that feels worlds away from the bustling cities. Visitors can take a boat ride through the winding waterways lined with mangroves, where the only sounds are the chirping of birds and the gentle rustle of the leaves. The forest is a birdwatcher's paradise, home to many rare and exotic species, and the calm waters reflect the lush greenery in a perfect mirror image. Exploring Tra Su offers a peaceful, meditative experience, where the connection between man and nature feels particularly profound. For those looking to escape the crowds and dive into Vietnam's natural wonders, this hidden gem is not to be missed.

7.4 Floating Markets and Village Life

Vietnam's rich and vibrant culture thrives not only in its bustling cities but also in its floating markets and traditional villages. These floating markets, mostly located in the Mekong Delta, represent a way of life that has existed for centuries. The villagers, with their close connection to the rivers and agriculture, create a distinct rhythm of life that fascinates visitors. Exploring these floating markets offers a glimpse into the daily lives of local traders and farmers, while village visits allow you to experience traditional crafts, local cuisine, and the gentle hospitality of the countryside.

Cai Rang Floating Market

Cai Rang Floating Market, located in the city of Can Tho, is perhaps the most famous and lively floating market in Vietnam. As the largest floating market in the Mekong Delta, it attracts visitors with its vibrant atmosphere where boats filled with fresh fruits, vegetables, and local delicacies cluster along the river. The market is best visited in the early morning when trade is in full swing, and the river becomes a colorful mosaic of boats. Visitors can buy fresh produce directly from the sellers, with prices ranging from less than $1 for tropical fruits to around $2 for a hearty bowl of pho or other local dishes served on boats. Cai Rang is accessible by boat from Can Tho, with tours starting at around $10 to $20 depending on the group size. A visit here is an unforgettable way to experience the dynamic pulse of life in the Mekong Delta, as the locals expertly navigate the waterways to sell their goods.

Phung Hiep Floating Market

Phung Hiep Floating Market, also known as Nga Bay, is another must-see market in the Mekong Delta region. Located in Hau Giang Province, this market is not just a place for trade but also a cultural meeting point where traditional village life is preserved. The market offers a wide array of products, from fresh produce to handmade goods and even exotic animals, such as snakes and turtles, which are sold as part of the local diet. Visitors can also find everyday household items and local delicacies such as banh mi and grilled fish for around $1 to $2. Phung Hiep is a bit less crowded than Cai Rang, providing a more intimate experience for those wanting to interact with local sellers and witness the slower pace of village life. To reach Phung Hiep, visitors can take a bus from Can Tho, followed by a short boat ride, with transportation costs averaging around $5. The authenticity of this market, combined with the warmth of the locals, makes it a great destination for those seeking a more immersive experience of the Mekong Delta.

Long Xuyen Floating Market

Long Xuyen Floating Market, located in An Giang Province, offers an authentic experience of the Mekong Delta, free from the tourist crowds that sometimes overwhelm more popular markets. This market is predominantly visited by locals, creating a genuine snapshot of daily life in the region. Long Xuyen's tranquil atmosphere is reflected in the relaxed pace of the boats that drift along the river, loaded with fruits like durians, mangoes, and coconuts. The prices here are often lower than at more famous markets, with a kilogram of fresh fruit costing as little as $0.50 to $1. Visitors can also enjoy a traditional breakfast of noodles or sticky rice for under $2. The best way to access Long Xuyen is by taking a bus from Ho Chi Minh City to An Giang, followed by a boat ride to the market. The quiet beauty of this floating market makes it a peaceful retreat for travelers looking to explore the Mekong Delta away from the crowds.

Vinh Long

The floating markets of Vinh Long, set amidst a network of winding rivers and lush green islands, offer a beautiful blend of market life and traditional village culture. Located in Vinh Long Province, visitors can explore both the vibrant floating market and the serene countryside where locals still practice age-old traditions like pottery making and rice wine distillation. At the market, boats loaded with tropical fruits and vegetables await buyers, while the surrounding village areas provide a glimpse into rural life. Visitors can purchase local products for around $1 to $2 and enjoy freshly made snacks while cruising the river. Vinh Long is easily accessible by bus or car from Ho Chi Minh City, followed by a boat tour to explore the market and nearby villages. With a price range of $20 to $30 for a full-day tour, it offers a perfect blend of adventure and cultural exploration, making it an excellent destination for those wanting to experience the dual charm of market and village life.

Cai Be Floating Market

Located in Tien Giang Province, Cai Be Floating Market is a charming destination that captures the essence of the Mekong Delta's cultural heritage. In addition to the bustling market where vendors sell fruits, vegetables, and flowers, Cai Be is also known for its traditional villages where visitors can witness the making of local crafts such as rice paper, coconut candy, and woven baskets. Food prices at the market are affordable, with fruits costing between $1 and $2, and street food like banh xeo (Vietnamese pancakes) priced at around $1. Cai Be is located about 80 kilometers from Ho Chi Minh City, and visitors can reach it by bus or private car for about $5 to $10, followed by a boat ride to the market. Day tours of Cai Be, which include visits to the market and surrounding craft villages, cost around $30 to $40.

CHAPTER 8
EXPLORING VIETNAM'S ISLANDS

8.1 Overview of Vietnam's Islands

Vietnam's islands are an incredible collection of diverse landscapes that offer an unparalleled experience for travelers seeking natural beauty, cultural discovery, and serene retreats. With their stunning beaches, crystal-clear waters, and rich marine life, these islands are a tropical paradise that has been captivating the hearts of adventurers and beach lovers alike. Scattered along Vietnam's expansive coastline, from the Gulf of Tonkin to the Gulf of Thailand, the islands vary in size and appeal, providing something unique for every kind of traveler. Vietnam's islands include Phu Quoc, Con Dao, Cat Ba, Cham Islands, and the Nam Du Archipelago, each offering distinct natural beauty and cultural experiences. Whether you are drawn to the quiet isolation of remote islands or the vibrant atmosphere of more popular destinations, Vietnam's islands will leave an unforgettable impression.

Unique Charms and Local Culture
Each island has its unique charm, with some offering tranquil environments perfect for relaxation, while others buzz with local culture and activities that bring travelers closer to Vietnam's vibrant coastal communities. The islands are also home to historical sites, fishing villages, and national parks, offering more

than just beautiful beaches. Whether it's soaking in the sun, diving into the rich marine life, or exploring traditional life untouched by time, these islands offer a diverse range of experiences to suit any traveler.

Convenient Access for Travelers

For those looking to explore, Vietnam's islands are easily accessible by plane, ferry, or boat, making it convenient to incorporate them into any travel itinerary. The islands vary in size, but each provides a unique snapshot of Vietnam's coastal beauty and culture. Whether you're exploring the remote and rugged landscapes or indulging in the comforts of luxury resorts, Vietnam's islands invite you to embrace both adventure and serenity. As travelers step onto these islands, they discover a side of Vietnam where time slows down, and nature's beauty unfolds at every turn.

The Rich Biodiversity of Vietnam's Islands

Vietnam's islands are not just a haven for beach lovers but also for those passionate about biodiversity. These islands harbor a wide array of wildlife, both on land and in the surrounding waters. Dense forests provide habitats for various species of birds and animals, while vibrant coral reefs lie beneath the water's surface, home to tropical fish, sea turtles, and other marine creatures. Visitors can embark on eco-tours to explore the islands' national parks and protected areas, offering a deeper connection to nature. These experiences allow travelers to witness Vietnam's efforts in conserving its natural treasures, making the islands not only a scenic destination but also a meaningful one for eco-conscious visitors.

A Blend of Local Culture and Modern Luxury

While the natural beauty of Vietnam's islands draws in adventurers, it is the blend of local culture and modern luxury that captivates a broader range of travelers. Fishing villages on the islands still thrive, providing a glimpse into traditional Vietnamese coastal life. Visitors can enjoy freshly caught seafood, visit local markets, or interact with fishermen who have passed down their trade through generations. At the same time, many islands feature upscale resorts, offering a luxurious escape with world-class amenities. From private beach villas to serene spa experiences, the islands cater to both those seeking authentic cultural immersion and those desiring a lavish, tranquil retreat.

8.2 Must-See Attractions

8.2.1 Phu Quoc Island

Phu Quoc Island is a gem in the Gulf of Thailand, nestled off the southwestern coast of Vietnam. Known for its pristine beaches, crystal-clear waters, and lush tropical landscapes, it offers a serene retreat that feels worlds away from the hustle and bustle of mainland Vietnam. As the largest island in the country, Phu Quoc has become a must-see destination for travelers seeking relaxation, adventure, and a taste of local culture. With its natural beauty and growing popularity, it is no surprise that this island is regarded as one of Vietnam's most treasured escapes.

Location and How to Get There
Phu Quoc Island is located around 45 kilometers from the Vietnamese mainland and is part of Kien Giang Province. Although it feels remote, getting to Phu Quoc is relatively easy. The most convenient way is by air, with direct flights from major Vietnamese cities like Hanoi, Ho Chi Minh City, and Da Nang. The island also has international connections, making it accessible from places like Singapore and Bangkok. For those preferring to take the scenic route, ferries and boats depart from the mainland town of Ha Tien or Rach Gia, offering a leisurely approach to the island.

Entry Fee and Accessibility

Phu Quoc has a special economic zone status, which means that most visitors can enter without a visa if they stay for less than 30 days, making it even more attractive to international tourists. There are no entry fees to visit the island itself, but certain attractions and national parks may have small fees for upkeep and preservation. Once you arrive, renting a motorbike or car is a popular way to explore the island, giving you the freedom to discover its hidden corners at your own pace.

Why Phu Quoc is Worth Visiting

Phu Quoc is a paradise that blends natural beauty with authentic Vietnamese culture. Its coastline, stretching over 150 kilometers, boasts some of the most stunning beaches in Southeast Asia, from the famous Long Beach with its golden sands to the more secluded Sao Beach, known for its white sand and turquoise waters. Visitors can lounge by the beach, take a dip in the warm waters, or enjoy water sports such as snorkeling and diving. The island is also home to an array of luxurious resorts that provide top-notch services for those looking for a more indulgent escape. However, Phu Quoc is not just about beaches. The island's interior is a verdant landscape of rolling hills, dense jungles, and pepper plantations. Phu Quoc National Park, a UNESCO Biosphere Reserve, offers hiking trails and opportunities to spot rare wildlife. Exploring the island's forests and waterfalls gives visitors a chance to connect with nature in a peaceful setting, far from the crowds.

Historical and Cultural Significance

Beyond its natural allure, Phu Quoc holds deep historical and cultural significance. The island played a vital role during the Vietnam War and was once home to a notorious prison camp where political prisoners were held. Today, visitors can tour the Phu Quoc Prison, known as Coconut Tree Prison, to learn about the island's darker past and its place in Vietnam's turbulent history. Culturally, Phu Quoc is also renowned for its production of fish sauce, one of Vietnam's most important culinary exports. The island's fish sauce factories offer tours, giving visitors insight into the meticulous process that goes into creating this pungent and prized ingredient. Additionally, Phu Quoc is famous for its pepper plantations, where you can see how black pepper is cultivated and harvested.

What to Do on Phu Quoc Island

There is no shortage of activities to keep you engaged on Phu Quoc. For nature lovers, hiking through Phu Quoc National Park or exploring Suoi Tranh Waterfall offers a refreshing escape into the island's lush greenery. Beach enthusiasts can spend their days hopping from one stunning shoreline to the next, basking in the island's sunny weather and warm waters. Diving and snorkeling are also popular, with many coral reefs surrounding the island. The An Thoi Archipelago, just south of Phu Quoc, is a haven for marine life and a great spot for underwater exploration. For a truly memorable experience, visitors can take a boat tour to the smaller islands around Phu Quoc, where the waters are teeming with vibrant sea life. Beyond natural wonders, Phu Quoc has a growing number of cultural attractions. The Dinh Cau Night Market is a vibrant spot to sample local street food, seafood, and buy souvenirs. Temples and pagodas dot the island, offering a glimpse into the spiritual life of its inhabitants. One of the most iconic spots is Dinh Cau Temple, perched on a rocky outcrop overlooking the sea, where locals come to pray for safety and good fortune.

A Culinary Adventure

Phu Quoc is also a food lover's paradise. From bustling night markets to beachfront restaurants, the island's culinary scene is diverse and mouth-watering. Fresh seafood is a highlight, with dishes like grilled squid, sea urchin, and crab served straight from the ocean. Don't miss the chance to try local specialties like herring salad, a traditional dish that showcases the island's rich fishing heritage. Phu Quoc's famous pepper also features prominently in many dishes, adding a unique local flavor to the food.

Practical Tips and Final Thoughts

Phu Quoc is a year-round destination, but the best time to visit is during the dry season, which runs from November to March, when the weather is perfect for beach activities and outdoor adventures. The island has a laid-back atmosphere, so casual clothing is suitable for most places, but it's always a good idea to bring a light jacket for cooler evenings or when visiting temples.

8.2.2 Con Dao Islands

Located off the southeastern coast of Vietnam, the Con Dao Islands are an archipelago of unparalleled beauty, history, and serenity. These islands are not only known for their crystal-clear waters, pristine beaches, and lush forests but also for their deep historical roots and cultural significance. Con Dao, once a place of tragedy, has transformed into a must-see destination for those seeking both adventure and reflection. The remoteness of these islands ensures that they remain one of Vietnam's hidden gems, offering a tranquil escape far from the hustle and bustle of city life.

Location and How to Get There
The Con Dao Islands are situated about 230 kilometers from Ho Chi Minh City. The largest island, Con Son, serves as the main hub for visitors. To reach Con Dao, you can either take a short flight from Ho Chi Minh City or Can Tho, both of which offer daily flights to Con Son Airport. Alternatively, there is a ferry service from the coastal town of Vung Tau, though it takes considerably longer—approximately 12 hours by sea. Despite the remote location, the journey is part of the adventure, offering stunning views as you approach the islands.

Why Con Dao is Worth Visiting

What makes Con Dao truly special is its combination of natural beauty and historical significance. The islands boast some of the most unspoiled beaches in Southeast Asia, making it an ideal destination for those looking to relax, snorkel, or dive in the turquoise waters. At the same time, Con Dao's past as a penal colony during the French colonial period and the Vietnam War adds a somber, reflective layer to any visit. The juxtaposition of this tragic history with the breathtaking beauty of the islands creates a unique travel experience that is both moving and restorative.

Historical and Cultural Significance

Con Dao's history dates back to the 19th century when it was used as a prison by the French colonizers to house Vietnamese political prisoners. Known for its harsh conditions, the prison system expanded over time, especially during the Vietnam War, becoming a notorious site of suffering and resilience. Today, visitors can tour the old prison sites, which serve as a testament to the indomitable spirit of the Vietnamese people. The Con Dao Museum provides detailed insights into the history of the islands, and a visit to the Hang Duong Cemetery offers a place for reflection, where many prisoners were laid to rest. This historical significance makes Con Dao more than just a tropical paradise—it's a place to honor the past while appreciating the present.

What to Do on Con Dao

Visitors to Con Dao can immerse themselves in both nature and history. The beaches here are exquisite, with Dam Trau Beach being one of the most popular. Its golden sands and calm waters make it perfect for swimming or sunbathing. Con Dao is also a diver's paradise, with its coral reefs teeming with marine life, including sea turtles and rare dugongs. Snorkeling and diving tours can be arranged through local operators, allowing you to explore the underwater world that remains largely untouched by mass tourism. For those interested in hiking, Con Dao National Park offers several trails through dense jungle, leading to waterfalls and panoramic viewpoints. This protected area is home to a variety of wildlife, including macaques, giant black squirrels, and rare bird species. The island's rugged terrain makes it an ideal destination for outdoor enthusiasts looking to connect with nature. Cultural and historical explorations should not be missed. A guided tour of the Con Dao prisons provides a sobering look into Vietnam's past, while the Lady Phi Yen Temple offers a more spiritual experience. Dedicated to a historical figure who is deeply revered by the Vietnamese, this temple is a peaceful spot for quiet reflection.

Entry Fees and Practical Information
While entry to the beaches and most natural attractions on Con Dao is free, there are small fees for entering the national park and visiting the prison museums. Con Dao National Park requires a ticket for access to its hiking trails, while the Con Dao Museum and prison sites charge a nominal fee. These small costs contribute to the preservation of the islands and their historical landmarks. Additionally, organized tours are available for those who wish to delve deeper into the islands' history and ecology, with prices varying based on the length and type of tour.

8.2.3 Cat Ba Island

Cat Ba Island, located in the northeastern region of Vietnam, is a hidden gem that beckons travelers with its raw beauty, captivating landscapes, and unique cultural experiences. As the largest island in the Cat Ba Archipelago, it sits at the edge of the UNESCO World Heritage Site, Ha Long Bay, providing a gateway to one of the most stunning natural wonders of the world. Despite its proximity to the more famous Ha Long Bay, Cat Ba Island offers an experience all its own—one that blends adventure, history, and an escape into nature.

Location and How to Get There

Located around 150 kilometers east of Hanoi, Cat Ba Island is easily accessible from the capital city. The journey typically involves a combination of bus and ferry rides, and for those seeking a seamless experience, there are also direct shuttle services that offer round-trip options. Visitors can first take a bus or private car from Hanoi to Hai Phong, Vietnam's third-largest city, which is approximately two hours away. From Hai Phong, ferries are readily available to take you to Cat Ba Town, the heart of the island. Alternatively, travelers can choose to cruise from Ha Long Bay, adding a scenic boat ride to their journey.

Entry Fee and Accessibility

For visitors entering the Cat Ba National Park, a nominal entry fee is required, which is used for the preservation and protection of the park's diverse ecosystems. This fee is approximately $2 USD, a small price to pay for the chance to explore such a unique and ecologically significant area. The island itself is very accessible to all kinds of travelers, with accommodation ranging from budget-friendly hostels to luxurious resorts, making it an attractive destination for everyone.

Why Cat Ba Island is Worth Visiting

What sets Cat Ba Island apart from other islands in Vietnam is its striking combination of natural splendor and vibrant cultural history. The island's rugged limestone hills, dense tropical forests, and crystal-clear waters create a sense of escape and adventure. But more than just its beauty, Cat Ba offers visitors a glimpse into Vietnam's rich history and traditions. It played an important role during the Vietnam War, serving as a strategic military base, and its history is still reflected in the remnants of old forts and war-era tunnels scattered across the island. For those looking to immerse themselves in nature, Cat Ba Island offers experiences that are unmatched. The island's unspoiled beaches, like Cat Co Beach and Monkey Island Beach, are perfect for relaxation, while its towering cliffs and lush greenery provide ample opportunity for exploration. Its central location within the Lan Ha Bay area allows visitors easy access to some of the most stunning seascapes in the world, with a fraction of the crowds seen in nearby Ha Long Bay.

Historical and Cultural Significance

The island's historical and cultural layers make it more than just a natural retreat. Historically, Cat Ba played a key role as a military base during the French colonial period and later during the Vietnam War. The relics of this time remain scattered across the island, adding depth to its appeal. Visitors can explore Cannon Fort, a military outpost that offers not only a fascinating glimpse into the island's war history but also panoramic views of the surrounding bay and karst formations. The island's culture is also deeply tied to its fishing communities. The traditional floating fishing villages, such as Cái Bèo, are among the oldest in Vietnam, and offer visitors a chance to witness a lifestyle that has remained largely unchanged for centuries. The resilience and simplicity of life on the water reflect the deeper spirit of the island, making it an authentic cultural experience.

What to Do on Cat Ba Island

Cat Ba Island is an adventurer's paradise, with countless activities for nature lovers and thrill-seekers alike. One of the highlights of any visit is trekking through Cat Ba National Park. Home to the endangered Cat Ba langur and a vast array of plant and animal species, the park is a protected area that covers over half the island's landmass. Hikers can choose from several trails that lead through lush jungles and up to spectacular viewpoints, such as Ngu Lam Peak, where the reward is a panoramic view of the island's limestone formations and sprawling forests.

Kayaking is another must-do activity, allowing visitors to explore the tranquil waters of Lan Ha Bay at their own pace. The bay's emerald-green waters are dotted with tiny, uninhabited islands and sea caves, offering opportunities for exploration that are both serene and awe-inspiring. For the more adventurous, there's rock climbing on the island's limestone cliffs, an activity that has made Cat Ba a renowned destination in the climbing community. For a more relaxed experience, spend time exploring the island's beaches. Cat Co Beach, divided into three sections, is within walking distance of Cat Ba Town and offers stunning views of the surrounding cliffs. Monkey Island Beach, accessible by boat, is more secluded and offers a chance to encounter the playful monkeys that the beach is named after. As the sun sets, the island's vibrant yet laid-back atmosphere comes alive, with cozy beachfront bars and restaurants offering the perfect spot to unwind.

Additional Information for Visitors

To make the most of your time on Cat Ba Island, it's essential to consider the best time to visit. The ideal months are from September to November or March to May, when the weather is mild and the island's natural beauty is at its peak. During the summer months, from June to August, the island can get quite crowded as it's a popular getaway for domestic tourists, but this is also the time when the weather is perfect for beachgoers and outdoor enthusiasts. In terms of accommodation, Cat Ba Town offers a range of options from basic guesthouses to more upscale resorts. For a more immersive experience, some travelers opt to stay on boats moored in Lan Ha Bay, waking up to the stunning beauty of the bay's towering limestone pillars.

8.2.4 Ly Son Island

Ly Son Island, often referred to as the "Jeju of Vietnam," stands as one of the country's hidden gems. Nestled off the coast of Quang Ngai Province, this island is a paradise of volcanic landscapes, turquoise waters, and a rich tapestry of culture and history. For travelers seeking an authentic Vietnamese island experience, Ly Son offers an unspoiled beauty that is hard to match. From its historical depth to its breathtaking natural scenery, this island captivates all who set foot on its shores.

Location and How to Get There

Ly Son Island is located around 30 kilometers off the coast of Quang Ngai, a central coastal province in Vietnam. Getting to Ly Son involves a two-step journey. First, visitors must travel to the town of Sa Ky, where they can catch a ferry. Sa Ky is accessible by car, bus, or train from major cities like Da Nang and Quang Ngai City. The ferry ride from Sa Ky to Ly Son takes about an hour, offering a scenic approach to the island as the waters shift from deep blue to shimmering turquoise. For those seeking more convenience, speedboats are also available, cutting travel time to about 30 minutes.

Entry Fee and Accessibility

Visiting Ly Son Island is a relatively affordable adventure. While there isn't an official entry fee to step onto the island, travelers should be prepared to pay for the ferry ride, which ranges from approximately 150,000 to 180,000 VND ($6.50 to $8 USD), depending on the type of ferry. Accommodations on the island are varied, with options ranging from budget guesthouses to mid-range hotels. The island is best explored by renting a motorbike, allowing visitors to easily traverse its scenic routes and secluded spots.

Why Ly Son is Worth Visiting

Ly Son's beauty lies in its volcanic origins, which have shaped the island into a dramatic landscape of black cliffs, white sandy beaches, and rolling green hills. What makes this island even more enticing is its lack of commercialization. Unlike other tourist-heavy destinations, Ly Son retains its raw and untouched charm. The island's coastlines are bordered by jagged rock formations formed from ancient volcanic activity, and these stark features against the blue sea are an unforgettable sight. For those looking to escape the hustle and bustle of city life, Ly Son offers a serene, tranquil atmosphere where nature and simplicity reign supreme.

Historical and Cultural Significance

The history of Ly Son Island stretches back centuries, with significant ties to Vietnam's maritime heritage. The island is known for its role in Vietnam's historical sovereignty over the Hoang Sa (Paracel) and Truong Sa (Spratly) archipelagos. This history is commemorated through the Hoang Sa Soldier Museum, which offers visitors a glimpse into the lives of Vietnamese sailors who defended these waters. Additionally, Ly Son is deeply rooted in spiritual traditions. Temples and shrines dot the island, such as the Duc Pagoda and the

Hang Pagoda, where locals and visitors alike can witness the religious customs that have been preserved over generations.

What to Do on Ly Son Island

Ly Son offers a wide array of activities that cater to nature lovers, adventurers, and culture enthusiasts alike. One of the island's most iconic spots is the Thoi Loi Volcano, now dormant but still awe-inspiring. Visitors can hike to the top of the volcano to experience panoramic views of the entire island, with the green farmlands of garlic fields stretching out towards the sea. Ly Son is famously known as "Garlic Kingdom," and a stroll through these fragrant fields offers a unique insight into the island's agricultural lifeblood. Don't forget to try the island's signature dish, garlic salad, a local delicacy made with fresh produce from the island's farms. For those seeking a beach escape, Ly Son's smaller neighbor, An Binh Island, is just a short boat ride away. Here, the beaches are pristine, the waters are clear, and visitors can enjoy activities like snorkeling, swimming, or simply lounging on the sandy shores. Additionally, Ly Son's coral reefs are some of the best-preserved in Vietnam, offering a snorkeling experience like no other, with colorful marine life and vibrant coral ecosystems just beneath the surface.

Cultural Festivals and Local Life

One of the most unique aspects of visiting Ly Son is experiencing its local culture and festivals. The island's residents are known for their fishing and farming traditions, and their way of life is simple yet deeply connected to the natural rhythms of the sea and land. One notable event is the Hoang Sa Soldier Feast and Commemoration Festival, held annually to honor the soldiers who safeguarded Vietnam's sovereignty over the Hoang Sa and Truong Sa archipelagos. During this time, the island comes alive with traditional performances, rituals, and communal gatherings, offering visitors a rare glimpse into Vietnam's maritime history and cultural pride.

Other Information Visitors Need to Know

While Ly Son may feel remote, it is equipped with basic amenities to ensure a comfortable stay. Travelers should be aware that the island operates on a slower pace of life, so conveniences like ATMs, large supermarkets, and luxury accommodations are limited. It's advisable to bring sufficient cash and essentials before arriving. As the island is small, exploring it by motorbike or bicycle is highly recommended. This not only allows for easy access to all the main sights but also gives visitors the freedom to discover hidden corners of the island at their own pace.

8.3 Hidden Gems of Vietnam's Islands

Cham Islands

The Cham Islands, located off the coast of Hoi An, offer a tranquil retreat into both nature and culture. Comprising eight small islands, the Cham archipelago is known for its vibrant marine life, coral reefs, and crystal-clear waters. The islands are part of the Cu Lao Cham Marine Park, making them a prime spot for eco-tourism activities like snorkeling, diving, and underwater photography. The islands' natural beauty, with their pristine beaches and clear waters, feels almost untouched, providing a rare opportunity to experience Vietnam's coastal ecosystem in its purest form. To reach the Cham Islands, visitors can take a speedboat from Hoi An, which offers a scenic ride across the sea. The main island also has a small village where visitors can experience the local way of life, from fishing to traditional crafts. Staying overnight in a local homestay is highly recommended for those looking to immerse themselves in the island's peaceful rhythm, away from the hustle of Vietnam's mainland cities. The Cham Islands' blend of natural splendor and cultural richness makes them a must-visit for anyone seeking to experience Vietnam's coastal gems.

Binh Hung Island

Binh Hung Island, part of the Cam Ranh Bay area, is one of Vietnam's lesser-known coastal treasures, often missed by tourists in favor of more famous destinations. Its untouched beaches, calm waters, and rocky cliffs create a postcard-perfect scene that feels worlds away from Vietnam's bustling cities. The island is known for its coral reefs, making it an excellent destination for snorkeling and swimming in crystal-clear waters. Beyond the beaches, Binh Hung's local fishing villages provide a glimpse into traditional life, where visitors can experience the warm hospitality of the locals and savor fresh seafood dishes. Reaching Binh Hung Island requires a short boat ride from the mainland, but the journey is well worth it for those seeking seclusion and natural beauty. Unlike more commercialized islands, Binh Hung remains a peaceful retreat with few modern amenities, allowing visitors to truly disconnect and enjoy the simple pleasures of island life. Hiking along the island's coastal trails reveals hidden coves and panoramic views of the surrounding sea, making it a paradise for nature lovers and adventure seekers alike.

CHAPTER 9
DISCOVERING VIETNAMESE CUISINE

9.1 Overview of Vietnamese Cuisine

Vietnamese cuisine is a delightful symphony of flavors that reflects the country's rich history, geography, and culture. It's a cuisine that draws inspiration from the land, the sea, and centuries of cultural exchange, blending local ingredients with culinary techniques borrowed from neighboring countries and colonial influences. For visitors to Vietnam, discovering the local food is not only a treat for the taste buds but an immersion into the heart of Vietnamese life. The food is light yet flavorful, with a harmonious balance between sweet, salty, sour, and spicy elements, often described as a cuisine that elevates simplicity to an art form. At the core of Vietnamese cuisine is the concept of freshness. Meals are built around fresh herbs, vegetables, and light broths, with a focus on using locally sourced produce. Whether dining in a bustling street market or an upscale restaurant, visitors will notice the importance of herbs like mint, basil, coriander, and perilla, which are often served alongside meals to be added to taste. The abundant use of herbs and greens not only enhances the flavor of dishes but also reflects the country's agrarian roots, where farming and rice cultivation have been a way of life for centuries.

Role of Rice in Vietnam cuisine

Rice plays a fundamental role in the Vietnamese diet. Grown in the fertile deltas of the Red River and Mekong, rice is more than just a staple—it's the backbone of daily meals. Whether it's served steamed as an accompaniment, turned into noodles, or wrapped in spring rolls, rice appears in various forms throughout the country. Visitors will quickly discover that rice-based dishes, such as "pho" (noodle soup) and "banh mi" (Vietnamese baguette sandwich), are iconic parts of the food culture, but there's so much more to explore beyond these familiar staples. Regional variations offer different interpretations of these dishes, giving travelers a taste of Vietnam's diverse culinary landscape.

Abundance of seafood

Vietnam's long coastline and network of rivers provide an abundant supply of fresh seafood, which is another cornerstone of its cuisine. From grilled fish in coastal towns to shrimp and crab in the Mekong Delta, seafood is featured in many traditional dishes. The fish sauce, or "nuoc mam," is perhaps the most important condiment in Vietnamese cooking. Made from fermented fish, it adds a pungent, salty depth to dishes and is often mixed with lime juice, sugar, and chili to create a dipping sauce that accompanies many meals. For visitors, this sauce may be an acquired taste, but it is integral to understanding the authentic flavors of the cuisine.

Street food indulgence

Vietnamese street food is legendary, and for many travelers, it's one of the highlights of their visit. Eating on the street, amidst the clatter of bowls and the chatter of locals, is an experience not to be missed. From the early morning markets to the late-night food stalls, street food vendors serve up delicious, affordable meals that capture the essence of Vietnamese cooking. Bowls of hot pho, plates of fresh spring rolls, and skewers of grilled meat are just some of the options that await hungry visitors. The street food culture offers a glimpse into the fast-paced yet communal nature of Vietnamese dining, where meals are often shared with friends and family, or enjoyed solo on the go.

Regional variations and influences

One of the unique aspects of Vietnamese cuisine is its regional diversity. Northern Vietnamese cuisine tends to be milder and more influenced by Chinese flavors, with an emphasis on clear broths and balanced seasoning. In contrast, central Vietnam is known for its bold, spicy flavors, often served with an array of vibrant side dishes. The southern region, shaped by the tropical climate, is marked by sweeter and richer flavors, with an abundance of coconut-based dishes and fresh fruits. For travelers, this means that as they journey from one region to another, they'll encounter a new array of dishes that reflect the local palate and ingredients.

The Dinning experience

Dining in Vietnam is not just about the food; it's a social experience. Meals are often shared, with dishes placed in the center of the table for everyone to enjoy. Visitors will find that Vietnamese people take great pride in their food, and it's not uncommon for them to invite strangers to join them at a meal, as sharing food is seen as a gesture of hospitality and warmth. This communal aspect of dining is something that visitors can embrace, adding to the overall experience of connecting with the local culture. For those with dietary restrictions, Vietnam's cuisine is generally adaptable. Vegetarians will find plenty of vegetable-based dishes, particularly in Buddhist communities, where meatless meals are common. The widespread use of seafood also provides alternatives for those who prefer fish to meat. However, it's important for visitors to communicate their preferences, especially when it comes to the use of fish sauce, which is often used as a seasoning in many seemingly vegetarian dishes.

9.2 Must-Try Dishes

9.2.1 Pho

Vietnamese cuisine is a vibrant tapestry of flavors, textures, and aromas, and at its heart lies pho—a quintessential dish that has captured the hearts and palates of food lovers around the world. This iconic noodle soup is characterized by its aromatic broth, rice noodles, and a medley of fresh herbs and meats, typically beef or chicken. Pho is not just a meal; it represents a rich cultural heritage and a beloved daily ritual for many Vietnamese people. Whether enjoyed at a bustling street stall or a high-end restaurant, pho embodies the essence of Vietnam's culinary identity and offers an unforgettable taste experience that invites visitors to savor every spoonful.

Where Pho is sold in Vietnam and Price

Pho can be found almost everywhere in Vietnam, from street vendors and local eateries to upscale restaurants. In cities like Hanoi, the birthplace of pho, you can find famous spots such as Pho Bat Dan, known for its flavorful broth and tender beef slices. In Ho Chi Minh City, visitors flock to Pho Hoa, a bustling restaurant that serves this beloved dish with an array of condiments to customize the flavor. Prices for a bowl of pho can range from as little as $1.50 at street stalls to about $5 in more tourist-oriented establishments. This affordability makes pho an accessible culinary delight for all travelers, regardless of their budget.

Tips for enjoying Pho

When indulging in pho, there are a few tips to enhance your dining experience. First, don't shy away from customizing your bowl with fresh herbs, bean sprouts, lime, and chili peppers, which add freshness and complexity to the dish. Each region in Vietnam offers its own unique twist on pho; for example, northern pho tends to be less sweet and more savory, while southern pho may come with sweeter elements and a wider variety of toppings. It is also essential to savor the broth before adding any condiments, as the intricate flavors are best appreciated in their pure form. Additionally, be prepared for a communal dining experience, as many pho shops have limited seating and may require sharing tables with locals and fellow travelers alike.

Cultural Significe of Pho

The cultural significance of pho extends beyond its delicious taste; it is a dish that embodies the values of Vietnamese hospitality and the importance of family meals. Many Vietnamese people enjoy pho for breakfast, and it often serves as a comforting dish during gatherings. The preparation of pho involves time-honored techniques, with the broth simmering for hours to develop its rich flavor. Many families have their own secret recipes passed down through generations, making each bowl a unique representation of personal and regional history. As you immerse yourself in the experience of eating pho, you'll find that it is not just a meal but a connection to the heart of Vietnamese culture.

9.2.2 Banh Mi

Vietnamese cuisine is a vibrant tapestry of flavors, textures, and aromas, with one of its most iconic dishes being Banh Mi. This beloved street food encapsulates the essence of Vietnam's culinary heritage, blending French colonial influences with traditional Vietnamese ingredients. The Banh Mi is essentially a baguette filled with a delightful medley of ingredients, making it a versatile and satisfying meal that can be enjoyed at any time of the day. As you wander through the bustling streets of Vietnam, the tempting aroma of grilled meats, pickled vegetables, and fresh herbs wafts through the air, inviting you to savor this mouthwatering delicacy.

Where Banh Mi is sold and price

The Banh Mi is most commonly sold at street food stalls, local markets, and small eateries throughout Vietnam, with each vendor offering their unique twist on this classic dish. In cities like Ho Chi Minh City and Hanoi, you'll find countless vendors selling Banh Mi, often with long lines of eager customers waiting to taste their creations. The prices for a Banh Mi can vary depending on the location and the fillings used, but you can typically expect to pay between 20,000 to 50,000 VND ($0.85 to $2.15 USD) for a satisfying sandwich. This affordability makes it a popular choice for locals and tourists alike, ensuring that everyone can enjoy a taste of this delectable Vietnamese treat. One of the most enchanting aspects of Banh Mi is its versatility. Traditionally, it is filled with a combination of meats, such as grilled pork, chicken, or beef, but vegetarian options are also widely available, featuring tofu or mushrooms. The fillings are complemented by a variety of fresh vegetables, including cucumber, cilantro, and pickled carrots and daikon, all of which add a refreshing crunch and vibrant flavor to the sandwich. Vendors often spread a layer of rich mayonnaise and a hint of chili sauce on the baguette, enhancing the overall taste. As a visitor, don't hesitate to ask for your sandwich to be customized according to your preferences, whether that means adding extra herbs or opting for less spice.

Tips for enjoy Banh Mi

When visiting Vietnam and indulging in Banh Mi, it's essential to keep a few tips in mind to enhance your experience. First, seek out busy stalls with a steady stream of customers; this often indicates that the food is fresh and well-prepared. Additionally, consider trying different variations of Banh Mi at various vendors to truly appreciate the diverse flavors that each region and vendor brings to the table. For those who wish to explore beyond the classic offerings, look for regional specialties, such as Banh Mi Xiu Mai, which features meatballs, or Banh Mi Thit Nuong, with grilled pork. Pairing your Banh Mi with a refreshing glass of Vietnamese iced coffee or fresh sugarcane juice can elevate the experience further. As you savor your Banh Mi, take a moment to appreciate not just the flavors but also the rich cultural history behind this beloved dish. The baguette is a remnant of Vietnam's French colonial past, while the local ingredients and preparation methods reflect the country's agricultural bounty and culinary traditions. By enjoying Banh Mi, you are participating in a vibrant tradition that connects you to the heart and soul of Vietnamese cuisine.

9.2.3 Goi Cuon

Among its myriad of dishes, Goi Cuon, or fresh spring rolls, stands out as a beloved favorite, cherished for its lightness, freshness, and the artistry involved in its preparation. These rolls, often referred to as "summer rolls" in Western contexts, encapsulate the essence of Vietnamese dining—fresh ingredients, minimal cooking, and an emphasis on balance and harmony in flavors. Made with rice paper wrappers and filled with a medley of herbs, vegetables, proteins, and rice vermicelli, Goi Cuon offers a delightful experience that tantalizes the taste buds while remaining health-conscious.

Where to find Goi Cuon an it's price

Goi Cuon is widely available throughout Vietnam, from bustling street food stalls to upscale restaurants. In cities like Hanoi and Ho Chi Minh City, you can find vendors specializing in these rolls, often set up at outdoor markets or food carts. Each vendor brings their own twist to the traditional recipe, allowing visitors to sample various flavors and styles. The price of Goi Cuon is incredibly affordable, typically ranging from 20,000 to 50,000 VND (approximately $1 to $2) per roll, depending on the fillings and the vendor. Some places may offer sets that include dipping sauces and sides, enhancing the overall experience. This affordability makes it easy for visitors to try this dish in multiple locations, providing a more immersive culinary journey. The beauty of Goi Cuon lies not only in its taste but also in its versatility. While traditional recipes often include shrimp, pork, or tofu, many vendors offer unique variations to cater to different dietary preferences. The fresh herbs—such as mint, cilantro, and basil—are what truly elevate the dish, providing aromatic bursts of flavor that complement the protein and vegetables. Dipping sauces, typically made from hoisin sauce, peanut sauce, or a tangy fish sauce blend, are essential for adding depth to each bite. Visitors are encouraged to experiment with different combinations of fillings and sauces, as this personal touch can significantly enhance the dining experience.

Preparing Goi Cuon

For those looking to try their hand at making Goi Cuon, several cooking classes are available throughout Vietnam. These classes often begin with a trip to local markets to source fresh ingredients, offering insights into the local food culture.

Participants learn the art of rolling the ingredients in rice paper, a skill that requires practice but is immensely rewarding. Engaging in this hands-on experience not only deepens appreciation for the dish but also allows visitors to take a piece of Vietnamese culinary tradition home with them. It is a delightful way to connect with the culture and meet fellow food enthusiasts.

Tips for enjoying Goi Cuon

When enjoying Goi Cuon, it is beneficial for visitors to be mindful of local dining customs. Eating with chopsticks is common, and many locals prefer to share a plate of Goi Cuon as part of a larger meal, promoting a sense of community and togetherness. Visitors should also embrace the casual nature of this dish; it's often enjoyed at outdoor tables or while on the go. This relaxed atmosphere adds to the overall enjoyment of the meal, encouraging diners to savor each bite while soaking in the vibrant street life that surrounds them. Whether you are dining in a humble street stall or a refined restaurant, experiencing Goi Cuon is essential to truly understanding and appreciating Vietnamese cuisine.

9.2.4 Bun Cha

Bun cha is a quintessential Vietnamese dish that embodies the rich culinary heritage of the country. Originating from Hanoi, this flavorful dish features a harmonious blend of grilled pork (cha) served over a bed of vermicelli noodles (bun) accompanied by a vibrant dipping sauce made from fish sauce, vinegar, and herbs. The dish is often garnished with fresh greens, pickled vegetables, and chili, creating a delightful balance of flavors and textures that capture the essence of Vietnamese cuisine. For visitors to Vietnam, indulging in bun cha is not merely a meal; it is an immersive experience that reveals the culture and traditions of the local people.

Where to Find Bun Cha in Vietnam

Visitors to Vietnam will find bun cha in numerous eateries and street food stalls throughout the country, but it is particularly renowned in Hanoi. The bustling streets of the Old Quarter are home to some of the best bun cha restaurants, where diners can enjoy this dish in its most authentic form. Local favorites include Bun Cha Huong Lien, made famous by President Obama's visit, and Bun Cha 34, known for its succulent grilled pork and flavorful dipping sauce. While bun cha is typically enjoyed as a lunch dish, many restaurants serve it throughout the day, making it easily accessible for visitors exploring the city.

142

Prices of Bun Cha

One of the most appealing aspects of bun cha is its affordability. A typical serving of bun cha costs between 30,000 to 60,000 VND (approximately $1.30 to $2.60), making it an excellent choice for budget-conscious travelers. Even in more upscale restaurants, the price remains reasonable, allowing visitors to savor this culinary gem without breaking the bank. Given its popularity, it is common to see long lines at popular bun cha spots, especially during lunchtime, so it is advisable to visit during off-peak hours to secure a seat and enjoy the atmosphere of the bustling streets.

Tips for Enjoying Bun Cha

To fully appreciate bun cha, visitors should embrace the local dining customs and experience the dish as the locals do. It is common to see diners slurping the noodles and dipping the grilled pork into the flavorful sauce, creating an intimate and enjoyable experience. Pairing bun cha with fresh herbs, such as mint and cilantro, enhances the dish's freshness and flavor, providing a delightful contrast to the rich pork. It is also recommended to try bun cha with a side of nem cua be, or crab spring rolls, which complement the dish perfectly and add an additional layer of flavor to the meal.

9.3 Hidden Gems of Vietnamese Cuisine

Cao Lau

Cao Lau is a dish deeply rooted in the history and culture of Hoi An, a city that was once a bustling trading port. Unlike other Vietnamese noodle dishes, Cao Lau noodles are thicker and chewier, made from local rice that is soaked in water from ancient Cham wells, giving them a unique texture. The dish is served with slices of pork, fresh herbs, crunchy croutons, and a small amount of broth, creating a rich, savory experience that balances texture and flavor. Its origins are believed to reflect a fusion of Chinese, Japanese, and Vietnamese influences, a reflection of Hoi An's diverse past. Visitors to Hoi An can find this dish at local street stalls and restaurants, each claiming to have mastered the perfect version of this beloved specialty. For any food lover, trying Cao Lau is not just about the taste—it's about immersing oneself in the living history of Vietnam's culinary landscape.

Bánh Xèo

Bánh Xèo, meaning "sizzling cake," is a crispy pancake that offers an explosion of flavors and textures in every bite. The dish is named after the sound it makes when the rice batter hits the hot skillet, and it's a delight to watch as it's prepared right in front of you. The pancake is filled with shrimp, pork, and bean sprouts, and then wrapped in rice paper or lettuce along with fresh herbs, creating a perfect blend of crispiness and freshness. What makes Bánh Xèo a hidden gem is its versatility—every region in Vietnam has its own variation, from the small, bite-sized pancakes in central Vietnam to the larger, foldable versions in the south. It's a dish that invites interaction, as diners must roll their own pancakes and dip them into a tangy, flavorful fish sauce. For visitors, trying Bánh Xèo is not just about savoring the food, but also about engaging in a hands-on dining experience that embodies the warmth and communal nature of Vietnamese cuisine.

Bún Riêu

Bún Riêu is a lesser-known but beloved Vietnamese noodle soup that offers a distinct and flavorful experience. Made from a tangy tomato-based broth, the dish is often topped with crab meat, fried tofu, and a variety of fresh herbs and vegetables. The sourness of the broth, combined with the richness of the crab and the lightness of the noodles, creates a complex, satisfying meal that's both comforting and refreshing. Although not as internationally famous as Pho, Bún Riêu is a hidden treasure of Vietnamese cuisine, offering an entirely different flavor profile that highlights the diversity of the country's culinary traditions. Visitors to Hanoi or Ho Chi Minh City will often find small family-owned eateries serving this dish, and its unique taste makes it a must-try for those looking to delve deeper into Vietnam's rich food culture.

Nem Lui

Nem Lui, a specialty from the central region of Vietnam, particularly Hue, is a dish that encapsulates the art of grilling. It consists of minced pork that's wrapped around lemongrass sticks and grilled over an open flame until smoky and fragrant. The skewers are served with fresh herbs, rice paper, and a special dipping sauce made from peanuts and hoisin, creating a perfect balance of flavors with every bite. What makes Nem Lui stand out is the role of lemongrass, which imparts a subtle, aromatic quality to the meat as it cooks. It's a dish that's typically shared among friends and family, as the process of rolling the grilled pork into rice paper wraps and dipping it into the sauce becomes a communal experience. Visitors to the central provinces, particularly Hue, should seek out Nem Lui for an authentic and hands-on dining adventure that showcases the bold flavors of Vietnamese grilling.

Bánh Canh

Bánh Canh is a unique Vietnamese noodle soup that sets itself apart from the more well-known Pho and Bun Bo Hue. Made with thick, tapioca-based noodles, the soup has a distinct texture that is soft, slightly chewy, and wonderfully satisfying. The broth varies depending on the region and can be made from pork, crab, or fish, but it is always rich and flavorful. What makes Bánh Canh a hidden gem is its adaptability—it can be found in various forms throughout the country, each version offering its own local twist. In central Vietnam, for instance, Bánh Canh Cua is a popular variation, made with a crab-based broth that is thickened with tapioca, giving it a hearty consistency. Visitors can find this dish at street food stalls, where the warmth of the soup and the thickness of the noodles provide a comforting meal, perfect after a long day of exploring. For those looking to experience the diversity of Vietnamese noodle dishes, Bánh Canh is a must-try that offers a new and exciting taste of Vietnamese comfort food.

9.4 Cooking Classes and Food Tours

Vietnam's culinary scene is as vibrant and diverse as its culture, making it a must-visit destination for food enthusiasts. Engaging in cooking classes and food tours offers an immersive way to explore the country's rich flavors and cooking techniques, allowing visitors to learn from local chefs and gain insight into traditional Vietnamese cuisine. These experiences not only provide valuable cooking skills but also create lasting memories of the local culture and customs. Whether you are a novice cook or a seasoned chef, participating in a cooking class or food tour in Vietnam is an adventure that deepens your understanding of the nation's gastronomic heritage.

Hanoi Cooking Center

Located in the heart of Hanoi, the Hanoi Cooking Center is a popular choice for travelers eager to dive into Vietnamese cuisine. The center offers hands-on cooking classes that teach participants how to prepare authentic dishes like pho and spring rolls. Classes typically last about three hours and include a visit to a local market to select fresh ingredients, followed by guided cooking sessions. Prices range from $50 to $75 per person, which includes all materials and a meal at the end of the class. For visitors, it's advisable to book in advance, especially during peak tourist seasons, to secure a spot in this immersive culinary experience.

Hoa's Cooking Classes

Nestled in the picturesque town of Hoi An, Hoa's Cooking Classes are designed for those who want a more personalized culinary experience. Participants start with a guided market tour, where they can interact with local vendors and learn about regional ingredients. Following the market visit, the class moves to a traditional cooking environment, where guests can learn to prepare various local specialties, including the famous cao lau noodles. Classes at Hoa's are priced at approximately $45 per person, and the intimate setting allows for plenty of interaction with the instructor. It is recommended to wear comfortable clothing and bring a camera to capture the beautiful setting and delicious dishes.

Saigon Street Food Tours

In the bustling streets of Ho Chi Minh City, Saigon Street Food Tours provides a unique opportunity for visitors to taste the local cuisine while exploring the vibrant city. These guided tours take participants through hidden alleyways and popular food stalls, sampling iconic dishes such as banh mi and pho along the way. Prices for these tours start at around $40, including tastings of multiple dishes and insights into the cultural significance of each. For a memorable experience, visitors should consider joining a night tour, when the city comes alive with street food vendors and lively atmospheres. Comfortable walking shoes are a must, as the tours often involve plenty of walking.

Red Bridge Cooking School

Another gem in Hoi An is the Red Bridge Cooking School, renowned for its picturesque location alongside the Thu Bon River. The experience begins with a boat trip to the school, offering a serene view of the surrounding landscape. Participants learn to prepare several traditional dishes, focusing on the fresh seafood and local produce that define Vietnamese cooking. The class lasts about five hours, with prices around $50 per person. The Red Bridge Cooking School also offers a unique culinary market tour, providing an authentic glimpse into the local food scene. Visitors are encouraged to take advantage of the scenic setting and explore the gardens surrounding the school.

Mekong Delta Food Tours

For those looking to experience the flavors of rural Vietnam, food tours in the Mekong Delta offer an unforgettable culinary adventure. These tours often include visits to local markets, traditional family-run restaurants, and cooking classes set in lush gardens. Prices vary, but visitors can expect to pay around $60 to $100 for a full-day experience, which includes transportation, meals, and cooking lessons. The Mekong Delta is famous for its fresh produce and unique regional dishes, such as river fish and tropical fruits. It's advisable for visitors to book tours that are small in size to ensure personalized attention and a more intimate experience with local food culture.

CHAPTER 10
IMMERSING IN VIETNAMESE CULTURE

10.1 Festivals and Events

Embracing the Spirit of Vietnam

Vietnam, a country rich in history and culture, celebrates a variety of traditional festivals throughout the year that reflect its deep-rooted customs and community values. These vibrant events offer visitors an opportunity to engage with local traditions, witness breathtaking performances, and savor exquisite culinary delights. Each festival is unique, providing a window into the soul of Vietnamese culture, making them must-see experiences for anyone traveling to this beautiful land. From the bustling streets of Hanoi to the serene landscapes of the Mekong Delta, Vietnam's festivals showcase the country's dynamic spirit and welcoming warmth.

Tet Nguyen Dan

Tet Nguyen Dan, or the Vietnamese Lunar New Year, is the most significant and widely celebrated festival in Vietnam, typically occurring in late January or early February, marking the beginning of spring. The festival lasts for several days, filled with colorful decorations, family gatherings, and festive meals.

Homes are adorned with peach blossoms in the north and yellow apricot flowers in the south, symbolizing prosperity and happiness. During Tet, locals prepare special foods such as "bánh chưng" (square sticky rice cakes) and "gio lua" (Vietnamese pork sausage), which are offered to ancestors as a sign of respect and remembrance. Visitors will find the streets bustling with markets selling festive goods, lanterns, and flowers, creating a lively atmosphere. Attending Tet is an extraordinary experience, as it not only offers a glimpse into Vietnamese customs but also emphasizes the importance of family, gratitude, and renewal as people come together to welcome the new year.

Hoi An Lantern Festival

Every full moon, the ancient town of Hoi An transforms into a magical spectacle during the Hoi An Lantern Festival, which usually occurs on the 14th day of each lunar month. The town is illuminated by thousands of colorful lanterns, casting a soft, warm glow over the cobblestone streets and the peaceful Thu Bon River. During this enchanting evening, visitors can partake in traditional activities, such as releasing paper lanterns onto the river, which symbolizes the release of bad luck and the welcoming of good fortune. The air is filled with the tantalizing aroma of local street food, as vendors offer specialties like grilled seafood and banh mi. Attending this festival allows visitors to step back in time, experiencing the charm of Hoi An while immersing themselves in the local customs and legends. The lantern festival is not only a feast for the senses but also a profound reminder of hope and renewal.

The Hue Festival

Taking place every two years, the Hue Festival is a grand celebration of the cultural heritage of Vietnam's former imperial capital, Hue. Typically held in April, this vibrant event showcases a diverse array of cultural performances, including traditional music, dance, and theatrical shows that reflect the rich history of the Nguyen Dynasty. Visitors can explore the imperial city and participate in various activities, from craft workshops to culinary tastings featuring royal cuisine. The festival also includes a spectacular parade along the Perfume River, featuring colorful floats and performers in traditional costumes. This celebration offers a unique opportunity for visitors to engage with local artists, experience ancient traditions, and appreciate the beauty of Hue's historical sites. Attending the Hue Festival is a chance to immerse oneself in the artistic soul of Vietnam, making it a truly memorable experience.

Buddha's Birthday (Vesak)

Buddha's Birthday, known as Vesak, is an important religious festival celebrated by Buddhists across Vietnam, typically occurring in April or May. This sacred event marks the birth, enlightenment, and death of Gautama Buddha and is observed with great reverence. Temples are beautifully decorated with flowers and lanterns, creating a serene atmosphere that invites meditation and reflection. Visitors will witness colorful processions featuring monks and nuns, chanting prayers and carrying offerings. In many cities, such as Ho Chi Minh City and Hanoi, public celebrations include cultural performances, lantern releases, and vegetarian feasts. Attending Buddha's Birthday provides a profound opportunity to experience the spirituality of Vietnamese culture while participating in a festival centered on peace, compassion, and community harmony.

The Mid-Autumn Festival

The Mid-Autumn Festival, known as Tết Trung Thu, is celebrated on the 15th day of the eighth lunar month, usually in September or October. This beloved festival is dedicated to children and family reunions, symbolizing abundance and happiness. Streets come alive with colorful decorations, and families gather to enjoy mooncakes, a traditional pastry filled with sweet bean paste or lotus seeds. In many towns, children participate in lion dances and parades, carrying glowing lanterns in various shapes and sizes, illuminating the night with a joyful spirit. The atmosphere is filled with laughter and music as families enjoy outdoor festivities, including games and storytelling. Attending the Mid-Autumn Festival allows visitors to connect with the warmth of Vietnamese family values and witness the joy of community celebration, making it a heartwarming experience.

10.2 Vietnamese Folk Traditions

Vietnam is a land steeped in history and culture, where folk traditions serve as vibrant threads in the nation's rich tapestry. Each tradition reflects the diverse beliefs, values, and customs of the Vietnamese people, offering visitors a glimpse into the country's unique identity. From colorful festivals celebrating the harvest to intricate ceremonies honoring ancestral spirits, these folk traditions are not merely events; they are living expressions of the collective spirit of the Vietnamese. For anyone intending to visit Vietnam, participating in or witnessing these traditions can provide an unforgettable cultural experience.

Tet Nguyen Dan

Tet Nguyen Dan, or the Lunar New Year, is the most significant celebration in Vietnam, usually occurring in late January or early February. This joyous occasion marks the arrival of spring and is a time for families to come together, honor their ancestors, and set intentions for the new year. Preparations begin well in advance, with families cleaning and decorating their homes, cooking traditional dishes, and making offerings to their ancestors. The vibrant streets fill with colorful decorations, markets brimming with festive goods, and the air is fragrant with the scent of blooming peach blossoms and kumquat trees. What makes Tet so special is its profound significance in Vietnamese culture; it symbolizes renewal, hope, and unity. Visitors during this time can participate in various activities, from joining in the lively parades featuring lion dances to indulging in traditional foods such as Banh Chung (square sticky rice cake) and pickled vegetables. The atmosphere is electric, filled with laughter, joy, and the warm spirit of togetherness, making it an essential experience for anyone wanting to understand the heart of Vietnam.

Hanoi's Mid-Autumn Festival

The Mid-Autumn Festival, known as Tet Trung Thu, typically falls in September or October, coinciding with the harvest moon. This festival is particularly enchanting as it celebrates children, signifying a time of family reunions and festive joy. Streets come alive with vibrant lanterns of all shapes and sizes, illuminating the night sky and reflecting the spirit of this joyous occasion. Families often prepare mooncakes, which are beautifully crafted pastries filled with sweet or savory fillings, and share them with loved ones and neighbors. One of the festival's highlights is the lively parades featuring children dressed in traditional costumes, carrying their colorful lanterns, and singing folk songs. The energy is palpable, and the smiles on the children's faces paint a picture of innocence and joy. Attending the Mid-Autumn Festival allows visitors to witness the deep-rooted cultural appreciation for family and the simple joys of childhood, creating memories that will last a lifetime.

The Buffalo Fighting Festival

The Buffalo Fighting Festival, held annually in September in Quang Nam Province, is a unique and exhilarating celebration that showcases the strength and skill of local farmers. This traditional event, dating back centuries, is not only a display of animal prowess but also a celebration of agricultural life and the community's bond with their livestock. The festival is marked by a series of buffalo fights where specially trained buffaloes compete in front of enthusiastic spectators, accompanied by traditional music and dances. What sets this festival apart is the deep cultural significance it holds within the local community. It symbolizes bravery and resilience, honoring the hard work and dedication of farmers. The atmosphere is filled with excitement as locals and tourists alike gather to cheer for their favorite buffaloes. Attending the Buffalo Fighting Festival provides an exhilarating experience that reflects the unique agricultural heritage of Vietnam, creating an unforgettable connection to the land and its people.

The Water Puppet Show
Originating in the rice paddies of the Red River Delta, the Water Puppet Show is a captivating art form that dates back over a thousand years. This traditional Vietnamese performance is usually held in the spring and summer, attracting visitors from all over the world. The show features beautifully crafted wooden puppets, manipulated by skilled puppeteers hidden behind a screen and maneuvered over a water surface. The performances depict various aspects of rural life, folklore, and legends, accompanied by traditional music and storytelling. What makes the Water Puppet Show so special is its ability to blend artistry, history, and culture into a mesmerizing experience. The puppets, adorned with vibrant colors and intricate designs, dance and play in the water, captivating audiences of all ages. For visitors, witnessing this unique tradition offers a glimpse into Vietnam's artistic heritage and the rich narratives that shape its cultural identity, making it an essential part of any journey through the country.

The Whale Worship Festival
The Whale Worship Festival, celebrated in various coastal towns across Vietnam, particularly in Phan Thiet, takes place annually in the second lunar month. This festival honors the whale, revered by fishermen as a protector of the seas. The event involves a series of ceremonies, including offerings, prayers, and processions, as communities come together to express their gratitude for the whale's protective presence and to pray for a bountiful catch. What makes this festival unique is its deep connection to the local fishing communities and their relationship with the ocean. Colorful processions and traditional rituals create a vibrant atmosphere filled with community spirit and reverence. Visitors attending the Whale Worship Festival can experience the profound respect that coastal communities have for nature and the importance of preserving their

traditions. This festival offers an enriching perspective on the interplay between culture and the natural world, making it a meaningful addition to any itinerary in Vietnam.

10.3 Arts and Music Scene

Vietnam is a country rich in history, culture, and creativity, where art and music intertwine to form a vibrant tapestry that reflects its diverse heritage. The artistic expressions found throughout Vietnam are as varied as the landscapes, from the bustling streets of Hanoi to the tranquil villages of the Mekong Delta. For visitors eager to immerse themselves in the local culture, exploring Vietnam's art and music scene offers an unforgettable experience. Each region boasts its unique artistic flair, showcasing the creativity and spirit of the Vietnamese people.

Contemporary Art in Ho Chi Minh City

Ho Chi Minh City, the bustling economic hub of Vietnam, is a melting pot of contemporary art that continues to evolve and thrive. The city is home to numerous galleries, art studios, and exhibition spaces where both established and emerging artists showcase their work. Notable venues such as the Saigon Contemporary Art Center and the Factory Contemporary Arts Centre provide platforms for innovative artistic expressions that challenge traditional norms. Here, visitors can explore a diverse range of mediums, including painting, sculpture, and mixed media installations that address contemporary issues and reflect the dynamic nature of urban life. In addition to galleries, the city hosts various art events and festivals throughout the year, such as the Ho Chi Minh City Art Exhibition, which draws artists and art lovers together to celebrate creativity and collaboration. Participating in these events offers visitors a chance to engage with local artists, understand their creative processes, and gain insights into the themes and narratives that resonate within Vietnamese contemporary art. Ho Chi Minh City's thriving art scene is a must-see for anyone wishing to connect with Vietnam's modern cultural expressions.

Traditional Music and Theatre in Hanoi

Hanoi, the capital of Vietnam, is a treasure trove of traditional music and performing arts that reflect the nation's rich cultural heritage. One of the most enchanting forms of traditional music is Ca Trù, a genre that combines poetry and music, often performed in intimate settings. The National Ca Trù Theatre in Hanoi is a prime location to experience this beautiful art form, where visitors can witness talented musicians and singers performing ancient folk songs, accompanied by traditional instruments such as the đàn đáy (three-stringed lute) and the trống (drum). Attending a performance here allows visitors to appreciate the intricate rhythms and poetic lyrics that capture the essence of Vietnamese culture. Another must-see performance in Hanoi is the Water Puppet Show, a unique form of theatre that originated in the rice paddies of the Red River Delta. Performed on water with puppets controlled by skilled puppeteers hidden behind a screen, this enchanting show tells stories of rural life, folklore, and legends, accompanied by live traditional music. The Thang Long Water Puppet Theatre is a renowned venue where visitors can enjoy this captivating experience. Witnessing the harmony of music and puppetry in this traditional setting provides a profound insight into the cultural roots of Vietnam, making it an unforgettable highlight of any trip to Hanoi.

The Richness of Folk Art in the Mekong Delta

The Mekong Delta is not only known for its picturesque landscapes but also for its rich tradition of folk art. The region is famous for its vibrant handicrafts, including silk weaving, pottery, and traditional lacquerware, each reflecting the creativity and skill of local artisans. Visitors can explore markets and workshops where craftsmen showcase their talents, allowing guests to witness the intricate processes involved in creating these beautiful pieces. Moreover, the Mekong Delta is home to unique folk music styles such as Đờn ca tài tử, a genre that combines traditional melodies with poetic lyrics. Often performed in local gatherings or at festivals, this music is characterized by its improvisational nature and emotional depth. Tourists can experience live performances in village settings, where locals gather to celebrate their heritage through song and dance. Engaging with the folk art and music of the Mekong Delta provides a deeper understanding of the region's cultural identity and fosters connections with the warm-hearted locals who take pride in their traditions.

Street Art in Da Nang

Da Nang, a coastal city renowned for its stunning beaches and natural beauty, has emerged as a hub for street art that breathes life into its urban landscape. The city's walls serve as canvases for talented local and international artists, showcasing vibrant murals that reflect the culture, history, and aspirations of the Vietnamese people. Notable areas such as the Han River Bridge and the 29/3 Park are adorned with striking artworks that range from whimsical depictions of daily life to thought-provoking social commentaries. Visitors can embark on a street art tour to discover the hidden gems scattered throughout the city, gaining insights into the artists' inspirations and creative processes. The art scene in Da Nang is not just about visual beauty; it also serves as a medium for social change and community engagement. By exploring the vibrant street art, visitors can connect with the city's contemporary culture while enjoying the fresh coastal air and the energetic atmosphere of Da Nang.

Cultural Festivals Celebrating Music and Dance

Vietnam is home to numerous cultural festivals throughout the year, each celebrating the country's diverse musical and dance traditions. One of the most notable events is the Hue Festival, held biennially in the ancient capital of Hue. This vibrant festival showcases traditional music performances, folk dances, and theatrical shows that highlight Vietnam's rich cultural heritage. Visitors can witness the grandeur of the royal court performances, featuring elaborate costumes and intricate choreography, all set against the backdrop of Hue's historic architecture.

Lunar New Year celebration

Another significant festival is the Lunar New Year celebration, where traditional music and dance play a central role in welcoming the new year. Local communities come together to perform lion dances, folk songs, and other cultural displays that celebrate the arrival of spring and symbolize good fortune. Attending these festivals allows visitors to immerse themselves in the vibrant atmosphere and connect with the local community, creating lasting memories that encapsulate the spirit of Vietnam.

10.4 Vietnamese Coffee Culture

Vietnam also boasts a vibrant coffee culture that is deeply woven into the fabric of daily life. As one of the largest coffee producers in the world, Vietnam has cultivated a unique coffee tradition that reflects its agricultural heritage and local preferences. The experience of enjoying a cup of Vietnamese coffee is not just about the beverage itself but also about the social interactions and cultural rituals that accompany it, creating a rich tapestry of flavors and experiences for visitors to savor.

The Coffee Growing Regions of Vietnam

The journey of Vietnamese coffee begins in the lush highlands of the Central Highlands region, where the country's best coffee beans are cultivated. This area is home to the Arabica and Robusta varieties, which thrive in the cool, mountainous climate. The terraced coffee plantations that blanket the hillsides create breathtaking vistas, inviting visitors to explore the fields where local farmers tend to their crops. Many farms offer guided tours, allowing visitors to learn about the coffee-growing process, from planting to harvesting. These experiences provide insight into the dedication and skill that go into producing high-quality beans, fostering a deeper appreciation for the rich flavors that define Vietnamese coffee.

The Art of Brewing Vietnamese Coffee
Vietnamese coffee is renowned for its distinctive preparation methods, particularly the traditional drip brewing technique that creates a strong, flavorful cup. The iconic phin filter is a staple in every Vietnamese household, allowing coffee enthusiasts to enjoy a freshly brewed cup at their own pace. Visitors can witness the brewing process firsthand in bustling street cafés, where the rich aroma of coffee fills the air. As the dark liquid slowly drips into a glass filled with sweetened condensed milk, anticipation builds for the first sip. The resulting brew, known as cà phê sữa đá when served iced, is a perfect blend of bold coffee and creamy sweetness. For those seeking a unique twist, trying cà phê trứng, or egg coffee, is a must. This decadent drink combines egg yolks, sugar, and sweetened condensed milk whipped into a frothy, creamy topping over hot or iced coffee, creating a delightful dessert-like experience. Exploring these brewing techniques and tasting the various preparations is a delightful way to engage with Vietnamese coffee culture.

Cafés as Social Hubs
In Vietnam, coffee shops serve as vital social hubs where locals gather to connect, unwind, and engage in conversations that can last for hours. The ambiance of these cafés ranges from rustic and charming to modern and sleek, each offering a unique environment for visitors to enjoy their coffee. Many establishments feature outdoor seating, where patrons can soak in the vibrant street life, surrounded by the sounds of bustling traffic and the laughter of friends sharing stories. Café culture is deeply ingrained in the Vietnamese way of life, with many people preferring to savor their coffee while reading, working, or simply people-watching. As you step into these inviting spaces, you'll find the warm smiles of the baristas and the rhythmic clinking of cups, all contributing to an atmosphere that encourages relaxation and camaraderie.

Whether it's a quick stop for a cup of coffee or a leisurely afternoon spent chatting with friends, these cafés are essential to the Vietnamese experience.

The Influence of History and Tradition

Vietnamese coffee culture is also shaped by the country's history and traditions. Coffee was introduced to Vietnam by the French in the 19th century, and it quickly became an integral part of daily life. Over the years, locals have adapted the brewing methods and flavors to suit their tastes, resulting in a unique coffee culture that combines traditional Vietnamese ingredients and techniques. The impact of historical events, such as the Vietnam War, has also played a role in shaping the coffee scene, as many cafés became gathering places for discussions and social movements. Today, visitors can explore the rich history of coffee in Vietnam by visiting historical cafés, such as Café Giang in Hanoi, where egg coffee was first created, or the iconic Café Lam, a favorite among intellectuals and artists. These locations not only offer a taste of delicious coffee but also a glimpse into the stories and memories that have shaped Vietnam's coffee culture over the years.

CHAPTER 11
OUTDOOR ADVENTURES

11.1 Hiking Trails and Nature Walks

Sapa – Fansipan Mountain Trek

Located in the northern region of Vietnam, Sapa is home to the legendary Fansipan Mountain, often referred to as the "Roof of Indochina." The trek to Fansipan offers breathtaking views of terraced rice fields, lush valleys, and mist-covered mountains. Visitors can access the trail from Sapa town, with various options for guided treks or cable car rides. The hike itself is challenging, but the reward is the stunning panoramic view from the summit. For those looking for a mix of adventure and scenic beauty, the Fansipan trek is a must.

Cat Ba National Park Nature Walk

Cat Ba National Park is nestled within the Cat Ba Archipelago, offering a serene escape from the bustling city life. The park's nature walk is a peaceful trail that winds through dense forests, limestone karsts, and diverse ecosystems. It's an ideal destination for wildlife enthusiasts, as the park is home to the endangered Cat Ba langur and a wide variety of bird species. Located just a short boat ride from Ha Long Bay, visitors can reach Cat Ba Island via ferry from Haiphong or take a scenic boat tour. The trails here offer a tranquil retreat into Vietnam's rich biodiversity.

Phong Nha-Ke Bang National Park
Phong Nha-Ke Bang National Park, located in central Vietnam, is famous for its karst mountains and extensive cave systems. The park's hiking trails lead through lush tropical forests, offering stunning views of the surrounding landscapes and access to the park's famous caves. Visitors can explore the area on foot, with guided hikes available to Son Doong Cave, the largest cave in the world. The park is accessible by car or bus from Dong Hoi, and entry fees vary depending on the length of the hike and cave tours. Phong Nha is an adventure lover's paradise, offering both natural beauty and thrilling exploration.

Ba Vi National Park
Located just outside of Hanoi, Ba Vi National Park is a popular destination for nature lovers seeking a peaceful retreat. The park's hiking trails wind through ancient forests, past hidden temples, and up to the summit of Ba Vi Mountain, offering breathtaking views of the Red River Delta. Visitors can reach the park by car or bus from Hanoi, making it a convenient day trip. The cool climate and scenic beauty of Ba Vi provide a refreshing escape from the heat and hustle of the city, making it a perfect spot for a leisurely hike and reconnecting with nature.

Cuc Phuong National Park
Cuc Phuong National Park, Vietnam's oldest national park, is located in Ninh Binh Province and is a treasure trove of biodiversity. The park's well-maintained hiking trails take visitors through dense rainforests, past ancient trees, and to caves that date back to the Stone Age. Cuc Phuong is easily accessible from Hanoi, and guided tours are available for those who want to learn more about the park's flora and fauna. It's a perfect spot for both casual walkers and more experienced hikers, offering an opportunity to experience Vietnam's oldest protected ecosystem.

11.2 Cycling Routes

Vietnam offers an incredible mix of scenic beauty and cultural experiences, making it a cyclist's dream. With its diverse landscapes, from towering mountains to coastal roads, cycling provides an immersive way to explore the country. Visitors looking to explore Vietnam's vibrant countryside and bustling cities on two wheels will find numerous routes catering to various skill levels and interests. These cycling routes are often accessible from major cities, with tour operators offering affordable bike rentals and guided experiences, ensuring a memorable journey for every traveler.

Hoi An to My Son Route

One of the most popular cycling routes in Vietnam is from the ancient town of Hoi An to the UNESCO World Heritage site of My Son. This scenic journey takes riders through lush rice fields, peaceful villages, and past rivers, offering a glimpse into rural Vietnamese life. The route is approximately 40 kilometers long and can be accessed through cycling tours that range between $20 and $50 per person. With well-maintained paths, this ride is suitable for both beginners and experienced cyclists looking to explore the cultural heart of central Vietnam.

Da Lat to Nha Trang

The route from Da Lat to Nha Trang offers cyclists an adventurous ride through Vietnam's Central Highlands, descending into the coastal city of Nha Trang. This 135-kilometer journey takes riders through mountain passes, pine forests, and coffee plantations, with breathtaking views along the way. The ride can be organized through guided tours, with prices ranging from $50 to $100, depending on the inclusions. Cyclists can rent bikes in Da Lat and make stops along the route to fully experience the region's natural beauty and local culture.

Hanoi to Mai Chau

Cycling from Hanoi to the rural valley of Mai Chau provides a tranquil escape from the city's hustle and bustle. The 150-kilometer route takes cyclists through scenic roads, alongside rice paddies, and past small villages where they can interact with ethnic minorities. This route is perfect for those looking to experience authentic village life and can be accessed by booking a guided tour, which typically costs between $70 and $150. The peaceful setting and welcoming locals make this a highly recommended ride for visitors seeking a cultural and scenic experience.

Mekong Delta Route

Cycling through the Mekong Delta is an unforgettable experience, with its winding waterways, floating markets, and lush landscapes. The flat terrain makes this route accessible for cyclists of all levels, and guided tours, ranging from $25 to $60, include bike rentals, local meals, and boat trips. The Mekong

Delta route typically starts in the city of Can Tho, offering travelers the opportunity to explore the delta's rich culture and natural beauty. This journey is not just about the ride, but also about immersing oneself in the daily life of Vietnam's southern region.

Hue to Phong Nha

The cycling route from the historical city of Hue to Phong Nha-Ke Bang National Park is both scenic and challenging, taking riders through small villages, farmland, and limestone mountains. This 200-kilometer route is ideal for more experienced cyclists, with guided tours costing between $100 and $200, depending on the level of service provided. The ride offers a deep connection to Vietnam's landscape and history, with stops along the way to explore ancient temples, pagodas, and local markets. It's a journey that combines nature, culture, and history, making it a must-do for cycling enthusiasts.

11.3 Water Activities: Kayaking, Rafting, and Fishing

Vietnam is a country that embraces its rivers, lakes, and seas, offering endless opportunities for water-based adventures. With its diverse landscapes, visitors can enjoy tranquil bays for kayaking, thrilling rapids for rafting, and quiet fishing villages along the coast. Whether you are a thrill-seeker or looking to relax, these activities provide an incredible way to explore Vietnam's natural beauty and cultural heritage. The following overview highlights where you can engage in these exciting water activities, how to access them, and other important details that will ensure a memorable experience.

Kayaking in Ha Long Bay

Kayaking in Ha Long Bay is one of the most iconic water experiences in Vietnam. This UNESCO World Heritage site, known for its emerald waters and towering limestone islands, offers serene conditions for paddling through hidden caves, lagoons, and floating fishing villages. Most visitors begin their journey from Hanoi, where transportation to Ha Long Bay is available via shuttle buses or private cars, with a ride costing around $10 to $20. Once in Ha Long Bay, many cruises offer kayaking as part of their packages, with prices ranging from $20 to $40 depending on the duration and tour inclusions. The entry fee for Ha Long Bay is typically included in these packages, and visitors are advised to wear comfortable clothing, sun protection, and bring a waterproof camera to capture the magical views.

Rafting in Phong Nha-Ke Bang National Park

For those seeking an adrenaline-pumping adventure, white-water rafting in Phong Nha-Ke Bang National Park is an experience not to be missed. Located in central Vietnam, Phong Nha is famous for its dramatic karst mountains and deep rivers that create thrilling rapids ideal for rafting. Visitors can access the national park from Dong Hoi, a city with regular buses and trains, and the cost of transportation from Dong Hoi to Phong Nha is approximately $5. Rafting tours are available for both beginners and experienced rafters, with prices ranging from $30 to $60 depending on the difficulty of the route and the length of the trip. The entry fee to the national park is around $12, but it is often included in rafting tour packages. Adventure seekers are advised to bring swimwear, sturdy water shoes, and a sense of excitement for this heart-pounding experience.

Fishing in Mui Ne

For visitors seeking a more peaceful and cultural water activity, fishing in Mui Ne provides a tranquil escape. Mui Ne, located along the southern coast of Vietnam, is a traditional fishing village that has become a popular spot for tourists. Fishing tours offer an authentic glimpse into local life, as visitors can join fishermen at sea or fish along the coastline. From Ho Chi Minh City, travelers can take a bus or train to Mui Ne, with transportation costs ranging from $5 to $10. Fishing tours typically cost around $20 to $50, depending on the type of experience and duration. There is no entry fee for the fishing tours themselves, but visitors may want to visit Mui Ne's famous sand dunes and beaches, where small entry fees of around $2 apply. Fishing in Mui Ne is an immersive experience, allowing travelers to enjoy the quiet rhythm of village life while casting their lines in the clear waters of the South China Sea.

Kayaking in Cat Ba Island

Cat Ba Island, the largest island in Ha Long Bay's archipelago, is a fantastic destination for kayaking enthusiasts looking for quieter waters and stunning natural beauty. The island is less touristy than Ha Long Bay, but offers equally breathtaking limestone cliffs, secluded beaches, and caves to explore by kayak. Visitors can reach Cat Ba Island via ferry from Hai Phong city, with transportation costs averaging $10. Kayak rentals on the island cost around $10 to $15 for a half-day, making it an affordable and flexible option for solo travelers and groups. There is no additional entry fee for kayaking, but visitors may want to explore nearby Lan Ha Bay or Cat Ba National Park, both of which require small entry fees of about $2. Kayaking on Cat Ba Island is perfect for

162

those who wish to paddle through peaceful waters while surrounded by untouched nature.

Fishing and Kayaking in Hoi An's Coconut Village

A unique experience combining fishing and kayaking can be found in Hoi An's Coconut Village, also known as Cam Thanh Village. This eco-tour takes visitors through coconut palm forests in traditional bamboo basket boats, offering an immersive look at Vietnam's coastal culture. Fishing tours here focus on traditional net fishing techniques, where travelers can join local fishermen and try their hand at casting nets. To reach Hoi An from Da Nang, visitors can take a 45-minute taxi ride for about $15 or a local bus for just $1. The cost of the fishing and kayaking tours ranges from $25 to $50, depending on the tour provider and inclusions. The experience also includes a visit to the coconut palm groves, where travelers can learn about local fishing techniques and even enjoy a fresh seafood meal. There is no separate entry fee, and the village tour offers an intimate connection to Vietnam's fishing heritage.

11.4 Winter Sports: Surfing and Rock Climbing

Vietnam may not immediately come to mind as a winter sports destination, but the country's diverse geography offers excellent opportunities for adventurous activities like surfing and rock climbing. From its long stretches of coastline to dramatic limestone cliffs, Vietnam has become a hidden gem for those seeking an exciting winter getaway. Although the weather doesn't typically drop to freezing temperatures, the cool, breezy conditions during Vietnam's winter months provide the perfect backdrop for adrenaline-pumping activities. Let's delve into two of Vietnam's top winter sports: surfing and rock climbing, and explore where and how visitors can get the most out of these thrilling experiences.

Surfing in Vietnam

Surfing in Vietnam is a well-kept secret that is beginning to capture the attention of international surfers. The best time for surfing in Vietnam is during the winter months, from November to March, when the northeast monsoon brings consistent waves to the country's eastern coastline. One of the most popular surfing spots is Mui Ne, a coastal town located about 4 hours from Ho Chi Minh City. Known for its long, sandy beaches and warm waters, Mui Ne offers waves that are ideal for both beginners and more experienced surfers.

163

Mui Ne is easily accessible by bus from Ho Chi Minh City, with tickets ranging from $5 to $10. Surfboard rentals and lessons are widely available at beachfront surf shops, with prices ranging from $10 to $25 per day for board rentals and $30 to $50 for a 2-hour lesson. There is no entry fee for the beaches, making surfing in Vietnam a relatively affordable activity. For those who want to experience surfing further up north, Da Nang is another surf hotspot, where beaches like My Khe and Non Nuoc offer similar conditions with breathtaking scenery. Da Nang is accessible by plane, bus, or train from major cities, and accommodation prices are budget-friendly, making it a great base for surf enthusiasts.

Rock Climbing in Vietnam

Rock climbing in Vietnam is an exhilarating activity that challenges adventurers to take on the country's stunning natural landscapes. The most famous destination for rock climbing is Cat Ba Island, located in Lan Ha Bay near Ha Long Bay in the north of Vietnam. Cat Ba offers limestone cliffs that rise dramatically from the water, providing both outdoor climbing routes and deep-water soloing, where climbers can scale the cliffs without ropes and drop into the water below. Winter months are ideal for climbing as the weather is cool and dry, perfect for gripping the rock To get to Cat Ba Island, travelers can take a bus or train from Hanoi to Hai Phong, followed by a ferry ride to the island. Transportation costs range from $10 to $20 for the combined trip. Once on the island, climbing tours can be arranged through local companies, with full-day guided climbing trips costing between $50 and $100 per person, including gear rental and transportation to the climbing spots. Entry to climbing areas generally doesn't require a specific fee, though hiring a local guide is highly recommended for safety and expertise. The dramatic cliffs and panoramic views of the bay make rock climbing in Cat Ba a bucket-list experience for adventure seekers.

Other Rock Climbing Spots in Vietnam

While Cat Ba is the most famous, Marble Mountains near Da Nang and Huu Lung in Lang Son Province also offer exceptional climbing opportunities. The Marble Mountains are a series of limestone and marble hills with several climbing routes that cater to varying skill levels. Located just 30 minutes from Da Nang city center, the mountains are easily accessible by taxi or motorbike, with transportation costs ranging from $5 to $10. For a small entry fee of $1 to $2, climbers can access the site and explore its caves and temples, in addition to rock climbing. Huu Lung, located about 3 hours north of Hanoi, offers a more off-the-beaten-path experience. This rural area features impressive karst formations, and climbing routes have been developed by local climbing enthusiasts. It's a quiet, scenic spot for those who want to combine the thrill of climbing with an authentic countryside experience. Accessing Huu Lung requires renting a car or joining a guided tour, with prices for day trips ranging from $30 to $60, depending on the service.

Why Surfing and Rock Climbing in Vietnam are Worth the Visit
Vietnam's winter sports scene is an exciting frontier for thrill-seekers. Surfing and rock climbing offer a fresh perspective on the country's natural beauty, allowing visitors to interact with Vietnam's landscapes in a unique and active way. The affordability of these activities, combined with the cultural richness of their surroundings, make Vietnam a fantastic destination for those looking to combine adventure with travel. Whether riding the waves on Vietnam's stunning coastline or scaling its towering cliffs, surfing and rock climbing promise unforgettable experiences for anyone visiting this dynamic country. With accessible transport, reasonable costs, and unforgettable locations, winter sports enthusiasts will find themselves drawn to the rugged beauty and thrilling challenges Vietnam has to offer.

11.5 Wildlife Watching: Birds and Animals

Vietnam's diverse ecosystems make it a haven for wildlife enthusiasts. The country's unique geography, with its mix of forests, wetlands, mountains, and coastal regions, creates an ideal environment for a wide variety of birds and animals. For those looking to experience Vietnam's natural beauty beyond the bustling cities, wildlife watching offers a chance to connect with the country's lesser-seen inhabitants. From rare bird species to endangered animals, Vietnam's national parks and reserves provide unforgettable opportunities to observe wildlife in their natural habitats.

Cuc Phuong National Park
Cuc Phuong National Park, located about 120 kilometers southwest of Hanoi, is the oldest national park in Vietnam and one of the most important sites for birdwatching in the country. The park is home to over 300 species of birds, including the critically endangered Delacour's langur and rare pheasant species. Visitors can take guided birdwatching tours or explore the park's numerous trails, which lead through ancient forests and limestone mountains.

Transportation to Cuc Phuong from Hanoi typically costs around $15 to $25 by bus or private car, and the park entry fee is approximately $2.50. The best time to visit for birdwatching is during the dry season from November to April when migratory birds flock to the park.

Cat Tien National Park
Cat Tien National Park, located in southern Vietnam about 150 kilometers from Ho Chi Minh City, is a UNESCO-recognized biosphere reserve teeming with wildlife. The park is known for its endangered species, including the Asian elephant, gaur, and the critically endangered Siamese crocodile. Birdwatchers can spot species like the Germain's peacock-pheasant and the endemic orange-necked partridge. The park offers guided tours, and visitors can also explore the forest on foot or by boat. Transportation from Ho Chi Minh City costs around $10 to $15 by bus, and the entry fee to the park is approximately $5. For those seeking a more immersive experience, overnight stays in park accommodations allow for nocturnal wildlife tours, where you might encounter nocturnal species like lorises and civets.

Bach Ma National Park
Bach Ma National Park, located near the central city of Hue, offers a cooler, misty climate that supports a variety of unique wildlife. With over 1,400 plant species and an impressive array of fauna, the park is home to the rare Indochinese tiger, leopards, and over 350 species of birds. The park's dense forests, rivers, and waterfalls create a perfect backdrop for wildlife watching and hiking. Visitors can access Bach Ma National Park from Hue or Da Nang, with transportation costing around $10 to $15 by bus or taxi. The entry fee is around $2.50, and guided wildlife tours are available for an additional cost. For the best wildlife experience, visit during the early morning or late afternoon when animals are most active.

Phong Nha-Ke Bang National Park
Known for its spectacular cave systems, Phong Nha-Ke Bang National Park is also an incredible destination for wildlife watching. Located in central Vietnam, the park is home to various species of primates, including the endangered Ha Tinh langur and white-cheeked gibbons. Birdwatchers will be delighted by species like the red-collared woodpecker and the sooty babbler, both of which are rare and found in the park. Phong Nha is accessible by bus or train from Hanoi or Hue, with transportation costs ranging from $10 to $25. The park entry

fee is around $6, and guided tours, which often include visits to the park's famous caves, can be booked for a more comprehensive experience. Trekking through the park's dense forests offers a chance to encounter its rich wildlife in a pristine environment.

Van Long Nature Reserve

Van Long Nature Reserve, located in Ninh Binh province just two hours south of Hanoi, is one of the largest wetland areas in northern Vietnam and a vital refuge for endangered species. The reserve is famous for being home to the critically endangered Delacour's langur, with less than 200 individuals remaining in the wild. Visitors can explore the reserve by boat, gliding through calm waters surrounded by limestone karsts and spotting wildlife such as water birds, otters, and reptiles. The cost of a boat trip is around $6, and the area is easily accessible by bus or motorbike from Hanoi, with transportation costing approximately $5 to $10. A visit to Van Long Nature Reserve offers a peaceful escape from the city and an opportunity to witness some of Vietnam's most elusive wildlife.

Wildlife Conservation and Responsible Tourism

When visiting Vietnam's national parks and wildlife reserves, it's essential to practice responsible tourism. Many of the species in these parks are endangered, and their habitats are fragile. Visitors should always follow park guidelines, respect the environment, and avoid disturbing the wildlife. Additionally, supporting local conservation efforts, such as wildlife rescue centers, helps protect these animals for future generations. By choosing eco-friendly tours and activities, visitors can contribute to the preservation of Vietnam's incredible biodiversity while enjoying unforgettable wildlife experiences.

CHAPTER 12
PRACTICAL INFORMATION AND TRAVEL RESOURCES

MAP OF VIETNAM

168

12.1 Maps of Vietnam: Hanoi, Ho Chi Minh City, and Key Destinations

Exploring Vietnam's diverse cities and landscapes requires proper navigation tools. Maps play a vital role in helping visitors find their way around key destinations like Hanoi, Ho Chi Minh City, and other notable locations. Whether you're wandering through ancient streets or seeking hidden natural gems, reliable maps ensure you stay on course.

Hanoi
In Hanoi, a tourist map is indispensable for uncovering its vibrant culture and historical sites. Digital maps help visitors explore famous spots such as Hoan Kiem Lake and the Old Quarter. Travelers can easily access these maps through apps like Google Maps or Maps.me for offline use.

Ho Chi Minh City
Ho Chi Minh City's bustling streets require precise navigation for first-time visitors. Digital maps provide essential information for exploring the city's landmarks, including Ben Thanh Market and Notre Dame Cathedral. Travelers can download detailed city maps from popular navigation apps or view offline maps for convenience.

Key Destinations
For those venturing into Vietnam's stunning countryside and coastal towns, digital maps are crucial. Places like Ha Long Bay, Sapa, and Phu Quoc are easily explored with detailed maps available through online platforms. Offline maps ensure seamless navigation even in remote areas with limited connectivity.

Digital Maps and Navigational Tools
Travelers can access maps digitally via apps like Google Maps, Maps.me, and CityMaps2Go. These apps offer downloadable maps for offline access, ensuring visitors have guidance at all times. Detailed directions, public transport routes, and real-time traffic updates are key features that enhance any trip.

Scan the QR Code for a Comprehensive Map
For a detailed overview of Vietnam's key destinations and attractions, scan the QR code provided in this book. This comprehensive digital map will guide you to every corner of Vietnam, ensuring your journey is smooth and well-planned. Every traveler benefits from having this essential tool at their fingertips.

12.2 Five Days Itinerary

For visitors with only five days to explore this captivating country, a well-planned itinerary allows you to experience the highlights while capturing the essence of its charm. Each day presents a unique opportunity to dive deeper into the heart of Vietnam.

Day One

Begin your adventure in the bustling capital of Hanoi, where the old and new collide harmoniously. Wander through the narrow streets of the Old Quarter, filled with lively markets and historical architecture. A visit to Hoan Kiem Lake provides a peaceful retreat in the center of the city, where locals practice Tai Chi at sunrise. The Temple of Literature, a symbol of Vietnam's rich academic heritage, offers insight into the country's reverence for education and Confucian values. As evening falls, take a walk around the lake, and perhaps attend a traditional water puppet show, an iconic Vietnamese art form.

Day Two

On your second day, embark on a journey to Halong Bay, a UNESCO World Heritage Site known for its emerald waters and towering limestone islands. Cruise through the bay, marveling at the thousands of small islets, many of which hold hidden caves and grottoes. Relax aboard a traditional wooden junk boat and enjoy seafood delicacies while surrounded by stunning scenery. Exploring the Sung Sot Cave or kayaking through hidden lagoons provides a closer look at the natural wonders that have made this destination world-famous. The tranquility of the bay, far removed from the city's hustle, offers a perfect contrast to the energy of Hanoi.

Day Three

On day three, travel to the historic city of Hue, located on the banks of the Perfume River. This ancient capital, once home to Vietnam's emperors, is steeped in history. The Imperial Citadel, a sprawling complex of palaces and temples, allows visitors to step back in time to Vietnam's royal past. Explore the elaborate tombs of emperors like Khai Dinh and Tu Duc, whose final resting places reflect the grandeur of their reigns. A traditional boat ride along the Perfume River offers a scenic route to the iconic Thien Mu Pagoda, a symbol of the city's spiritual depth.

Day Four

Next, travel south to the charming town of Hoi An, a well-preserved trading port known for its unique blend of architecture and cultural influences. The town's narrow streets are lined with ancient temples, Chinese merchant houses, and French colonial buildings. Wander through the Lantern Market as the sun sets, where the town is bathed in the glow of colorful lanterns that light up the night sky. Hoi An's cuisine is another highlight, with dishes like Cao Lau and Banh Mi offering a delicious taste of local flavors. Visitors can also participate in a cooking class or visit the local tailors, famous for their craftsmanship in making bespoke clothing.

Day Five

Travel to Ho Chi Minh City, formerly known as Saigon. This vibrant metropolis is the commercial hub of Vietnam, with a dynamic energy that pulses through its streets. Visit the War Remnants Museum for a sobering reflection on the country's tumultuous past, then explore the French colonial landmarks such as the Notre-Dame Cathedral and the Central Post Office. In the afternoon, take a short trip outside the city to the Cu Chi Tunnels, a vast underground network used by the Viet Cong during the Vietnam War. Crawling through the tunnels offers a poignant glimpse into the resilience and resourcefulness of those who lived through the war. Return to Saigon for a final evening enjoying the lively nightlife, from rooftop bars to bustling street food markets.

12.3 Safety Tips and Emergency Contacts

Traveling in Vietnam is generally safe, but as with any destination, being aware of your surroundings and knowing important safety measures can ensure a smooth and enjoyable trip. It is important to stay cautious when navigating crowded areas like markets or tourist hotspots, where pickpocketing may occur. Securing your belongings, especially in public transportation and busy streets, helps prevent petty theft. Additionally, always be mindful of traffic, as motorbikes dominate the roads, and crossing streets can be challenging, especially in urban centers.

Emergency contact in Vietnam

For emergency situations, knowing key contacts is crucial for peace of mind. Vietnam's national emergency numbers provide quick assistance; the police can be reached at 113, fire services at 114, and medical emergencies at 115. It is recommended that visitors have these numbers saved in their phones upon arrival. Hospitals in major cities, such as Hanoi and Ho Chi Minh City, typically have English-speaking staff and offer international-standard care. Private hospitals may be the best option for expatriates or tourists requiring urgent medical attention.

Emergency services and medical assistance

In addition to being aware of emergency contacts, staying healthy and safe involves taking certain health precautions. Make sure your vaccinations are up to date, especially for diseases like Hepatitis A and Typhoid, which are prevalent in parts of Southeast Asia. Carry a basic first aid kit, including medicine for common issues like digestive problems, as food and water conditions may differ from what you are used to. Bottled water is widely available and should be used instead of tap water to avoid potential stomach issues.

Staying connected

Staying connected is another critical aspect of ensuring safety. Purchasing a local SIM card is easy and provides affordable access to data, allowing you to stay in touch with family or use GPS in unfamiliar areas. Wi-Fi is also widely available in cafes, hotels, and public spaces, so staying connected won't be an issue in major towns and cities. Being reachable in case of emergencies not only helps in critical situations but also provides ease for coordination and navigation during your stay.

General precautions and tips for travelers

While Vietnam is a safe and welcoming country, it is wise to have a contingency plan for any unexpected issues. Travel insurance is highly recommended, as it provides coverage for accidents, medical emergencies, and trip cancellations. Whether it's a minor health issue or an unexpected incident, having comprehensive travel insurance can give you peace of mind during your adventure in Vietnam. Being prepared with these safety tips and contacts will ensure that you enjoy the vibrant culture and beauty of Vietnam without any undue stress.

12.4 Shopping and Souvenirs

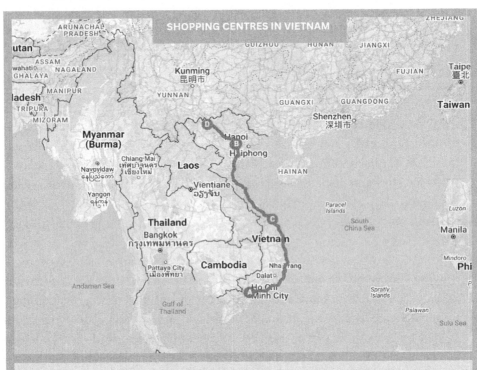

Directions from Ben Thanh Market, Bến Thành, District 1, Ho Chi Minh City, Vietnam to Van Phúc silk village, Hà Đông, Hanoi, Vietnam

A
Ben Thanh Market, Bến Thành, District 1, Ho Chi Minh City, Vietnam

B
Đồng Xuân Market, Old Quarter, Dong Xuan, Hoàn Kilim, Hanoi, Vietnam

C
Hội An Night Market, Nguyên Hoàng, An Hội, Minh An, Hội An, Quảng Nam, Vietnam

D
Sapa Night Market, Lương Định Của, Sa Pa, Lào Cai, Vietnam

E
Binh Tay Market, Tháp Mười, Phường 2, District 6, Ho Chi Minh City, Vietnam

F
Vạn Phúc silk village, Hà Đông, Hanoi, Vietnam

173

Shopping in Vietnam offers a delightful experience, blending vibrant markets with traditional craftsmanship and modern malls, as such, visitors will find a range of local products that make for memorable souvenirs. From intricately crafted items to flavorful delights, shopping in Vietnam is an adventure filled with surprises at every corner.

Ben Thanh Market, Ho Chi Minh City

Ben Thanh Market is one of the most iconic shopping destinations in Ho Chi Minh City, offering a wide variety of products ranging from clothing to handicrafts. Located in District 1, this bustling market is easily accessible by taxi or motorbike, making it a popular spot for both locals and tourists. Visitors can find traditional silk garments, lacquerware, and local coffee among the stalls, with prices that can be bargained down for the best deal. The market is not only a place to shop but also a cultural experience, where the lively energy and colorful displays capture the vibrancy of the city.

Dong Xuan Market, Hanoi

Situated in the heart of Hanoi's Old Quarter, Dong Xuan Market is known for its wide range of goods, including textiles, electronics, and souvenirs. This historic indoor market has been serving shoppers since the French colonial period and remains a favorite spot for both locals and tourists. Visitors can explore the narrow alleys filled with vibrant fabrics, handicrafts, and traditional hats, while soaking in the bustling atmosphere. The market is easily accessible from major hotels in the Old Quarter, with taxis and motorbikes being the most common modes of transportation.

Hoi An Night Market, Hoi An

The Hoi An Night Market, located along the Thu Bon River, is a must-visit for those seeking unique souvenirs in a charming setting. Known for its lanterns, the market comes alive in the evening with a magical glow that creates an enchanting shopping experience. Visitors can purchase handcrafted lanterns, ceramics, and jewelry, all made by local artisans, as well as sample street food while wandering the stalls. The market is within walking distance from Hoi An's ancient town, making it convenient for visitors staying nearby to explore.

Sapa Market, Sapa

Sapa Market is a treasure trove of local handicrafts and ethnic textiles, set against the backdrop of the stunning Sapa mountains in northern Vietnam. The market, located near the town's central square, is accessible by foot from most accommodations in Sapa and offers an array of colorful fabrics, traditional clothing, and handmade jewelry. It is an excellent place to pick up embroidered bags, blankets, and other items made by the ethnic minorities in the region, providing a meaningful way to support local communities.

Binh Tay Market, Ho Chi Minh City

Binh Tay Market, situated in the heart of Ho Chi Minh City's Chinatown, is a bustling market that offers a wide range of products, from fresh produce to souvenirs. Located in District 6, this market is less touristy than Ben Thanh, making it an ideal spot for those looking for authentic local shopping experiences. Visitors can explore aisles filled with traditional Vietnamese hats, bamboo products, and spices, with many vendors speaking little English, so bargaining becomes part of the fun. Getting here by taxi or motorbike is recommended, as the market can be busy during peak hours.

Van Phuc Silk Village, Hanoi

Van Phuc Silk Village, located just 10 kilometers from Hanoi's city center, is a charming destination known for its high-quality silk products. Visitors can find a wide range of silk items, from scarves to dresses, all handcrafted by skilled artisans who have passed down their knowledge for generations. The village is easily accessible by taxi or bus, and many tourists enjoy the opportunity to visit the workshops where the silk is woven. Purchasing a silk product from Van Phuc is not only a wonderful souvenir but also a way to connect with Vietnam's rich textile heritage.

12.5 Useful Websites, Mobile Apps, and Online Resources

Navigating Vietnam as a visitor has become much more convenient with the rise of useful websites, mobile apps, and online resources. Whether you're looking for travel guides, maps, or transportation options, having the right digital tools can enhance your experience. These resources ensure that travelers have all the essential information at their fingertips, from hotel bookings to local attractions, making every journey seamless and enjoyable.

Vietnam Tourism Official Website

The Vietnam Tourism official website (https://vietnam.travel/) offers comprehensive information about key destinations, travel tips, and cultural insights. It's a great starting point for visitors to learn about must-see attractions, festivals, and local customs. The website also provides up-to-date information on travel restrictions and safety guidelines, making it essential for planning.

Google Maps

Google Maps (https://maps.google.com/) is an invaluable tool for navigating Vietnam's cities and rural areas. It provides accurate routes, live traffic updates, and public transportation options. The app can be used offline in case of limited internet access, making it a reliable companion for both urban exploration and off-the-beaten-path adventures.

Grab

Grab (https://www.grab.com/) is Vietnam's leading ride-hailing and food delivery app, offering an efficient way to get around major cities like Hanoi and Ho Chi Minh City. Visitors can use the app to book taxis, motorbike rides, or order meals, with transparent pricing and easy cashless payments. Grab also provides airport transfers and other travel services, ensuring convenience for tourists.

Airbnb

Airbnb (https://www.airbnb.com/) is a popular platform for booking unique accommodations across Vietnam, from city apartments to beachfront villas. It allows visitors to choose from a wide variety of lodging options, offering more personal and local experiences compared to traditional hotels. The app provides secure booking options, guest reviews, and detailed property descriptions.

Foody

Foody (https://www.foody.vn/) is Vietnam's top food discovery platform, featuring reviews, menus, and ratings of restaurants and street food vendors. It helps travelers explore the diverse culinary landscape, from fine dining to local street food gems. The app also allows users to make reservations or order food for delivery, providing easy access to Vietnam's rich flavors.

Vietnam Airlines Official Website

Vietnam Airlines (https://www.vietnamairlines.com/) is the national carrier's official platform, providing details on flights, bookings, and travel promotions. Visitors can check flight schedules, book tickets, and access travel information all in one place. It's a vital resource for those traveling domestically or internationally in and out of Vietnam.

Zalo

Zalo (https://zalo.me/) is a popular messaging app used widely by locals for communication, making it a great tool for staying in touch during your visit. With Zalo, travelers can easily communicate with local contacts, businesses, or tour guides. It offers voice calls, text messaging, and even location sharing, ensuring you're always connected.

Booking.com

Booking.com (https://www.booking.com/) is an excellent resource for finding accommodations throughout Vietnam, offering a wide range of hotels, hostels, and guesthouses. Visitors can easily compare prices, read reviews, and book accommodations tailored to their preferences. The platform also offers deals and last-minute booking options, ensuring flexibility.

Currency Converter App

A reliable currency converter app, such as XE Currency (https://www.xe.com/), is essential for travelers navigating Vietnam's currency, the Vietnamese dong. This app provides up-to-date exchange rates and helps visitors manage their budgets. It works offline, making it especially useful in areas with limited connectivity or when making purchases in local markets.

12.6 Internet Access and Connectivity

In recent years, Vietnam has become increasingly connected to the digital world, offering reliable internet access to both locals and visitors. Whether in the bustling cities of Hanoi or Ho Chi Minh City, or in more rural areas, travelers will find that staying connected is easier than ever. The widespread availability of Wi-Fi in hotels, cafes, and restaurants ensures that visitors can seamlessly access the internet for work or leisure. Vietnam's growing digital infrastructure means that tourists can navigate their way through the country without worrying about communication barriers.

Wi-Fi Availability Across the Country

Wi-Fi connectivity in Vietnam is impressively widespread, especially in urban centers. Cafes, eateries, and even street food vendors often provide free Wi-Fi, making it easy for visitors to stay connected while on the move. Hotels and guesthouses, regardless of their rating, typically offer free Wi-Fi as part of their amenities. This convenience allows travelers to keep in touch with loved ones, explore tourist destinations online, or simply relax with streaming services during their stay.

Mobile Data Networks and SIM Cards

For those who need constant connectivity while traveling, purchasing a local SIM card is a popular option in Vietnam. The country boasts several mobile providers that offer affordable prepaid data plans. With 4G and now 5G coverage expanding across the nation, mobile internet speeds are generally fast and reliable. Visitors can purchase SIM cards easily at the airport, convenience stores, or local vendors, ensuring they can access mobile data wherever their journey takes them.

Rural and Remote Areas Connectivity

While Vietnam's cities offer extensive connectivity, internet access in rural or mountainous regions may be less consistent. However, even in remote areas like the highlands of Sapa or the Mekong Delta, tourists will find that most accommodations still provide basic Wi-Fi services. Travelers venturing into these less populated areas should be prepared for slower internet speeds or brief disruptions, especially during adverse weather conditions. Nonetheless, the connectivity remains functional enough for essential communications.

Public Internet and Internet Cafes

In addition to mobile data and hotel Wi-Fi, visitors can also find internet access in public spaces and internet cafes. Although internet cafes are becoming less common due to the rise of smartphones, they can still be found in smaller towns or rural regions. These cafes often cater to younger audiences for gaming but can be a reliable option for tourists needing quick access to the web. With affordable prices, internet cafes can be a handy solution for those without data plans or personal devices.

Vietnam's Online Freedom and Safety

When it comes to internet safety and online freedom, Vietnam has certain restrictions on content, particularly in terms of political discussions. Websites or content critical of the government may be blocked. However, for tourists seeking information on travel, entertainment, or general browsing, these restrictions are rarely an issue. It is advisable to use VPN services for unrestricted access to the global web, especially if you need to access certain services or websites blocked within the country.

12.7 Visitor Centers and Tourist Assistance

Vietnam offers numerous visitor centers that provide essential information to travelers. These centers are located in major cities and tourist hubs, offering maps, brochures, and advice on navigating the area. Visitors can seek assistance for bookings, tours, and any other travel-related inquiries they may have during their stay.

Hanoi Tourist Information Center

Located at 28 Hang Dau Street, Hoan Kiem, the Hanoi Tourist Information Center is the main hub for visitors to the capital city. It provides information on attractions, accommodations, and transportation. Visitors can explore more details through their website at https://vietnamtourism.gov.vn/.

Ho Chi Minh City Tourist Information Center

Situated at 88 Dong Khoi Street in District 1, the Ho Chi Minh City Tourist Information Center serves as a primary resource for exploring southern Vietnam. The staff here assists with itinerary planning and local recommendations. Visit https://www.visithcmc.vn/ for more details.

Da Nang Visitor Center

The Da Nang Visitor Center, located at 108 Bach Dang Street, provides travelers with information on central Vietnam, including nearby beaches and historic sites. They offer multilingual services for international visitors. For further information, visit https://linkbio.co/danangvisitorcenter.

Sapa Tourist Information Center

Located at 2 Fansipan Road, Sapa's Tourist Information Center assists visitors with exploring the Northern Highlands. They provide tips on trekking, local markets, and cultural experiences. For more details, visit their website at https://sapa-tourism.com/.

Hue Tourist Information Center

At 45 Le Loi Street, the Hue Tourist Information Center offers insights into the city's rich imperial history. Visitors can get information on the citadel, royal tombs, and other cultural sites.

CONCLUSION AND RECOMMENDATIONS

As you reach the end of this guide, I hope the journey through the rich landscapes, vibrant cities, and hidden corners of Vietnam has sparked within you a deep sense of wonder and curiosity. Vietnam is more than a country; it is a tapestry of experiences woven through its stunning natural beauty, ancient traditions, and modern growth. Whether you are seeking adventure, history, culture, or relaxation, Vietnam offers it all in abundance. But beyond the destinations, the true magic of Vietnam lies in the warmth of its people, the stories they share, and the life-changing memories you will carry long after your visit. In this book, I've strived to introduce you to the essence of Vietnam, from the misty mountains of Sapa to the sprawling delta of the Mekong River, from the chaotic buzz of Ho Chi Minh City to the serene beauty of Ha Long Bay. But no guidebook can fully capture the sensations that will greet you when you step foot in this country. The smell of fresh herbs and spices from street vendors, the sounds of bustling markets, the awe of standing before ancient temples—all of this awaits your discovery. I encourage you to embrace the journey ahead with an open heart and an adventurous spirit, for Vietnam is a country that rewards those who are willing to explore its layers.

Vietnam is a place where the past and future coexist harmoniously. Its ancient traditions, such as Tet celebrations and folk performances, will take you back in time, while its growing cities will plunge you into a world of modernity and progress. The balance between these two worlds is delicate, and experiencing both sides of Vietnam is what makes a visit here so transformative. The resilience of the Vietnamese people, shaped by their long and complex history, will leave you with a newfound respect for their culture and a deeper appreciation for their way of life. If there is one recommendation I can leave you with, it is this: take your time. Do not rush through Vietnam with the sole aim of ticking off destinations on a map. Instead, linger in the quiet moments, strike up conversations with locals, and let the country reveal itself to you naturally. Whether you're enjoying a bowl of *pho* in a small café, wandering through ancient pagodas, or cycling through rice paddies, the richness of Vietnam is best experienced slowly and mindfully. In doing so, you will find that every moment in Vietnam has the potential to become a cherished memory.

Another important recommendation is to embrace the diversity of Vietnam's regions. The northern, central, and southern parts of the country are all unique in their geography, culture, and food. Don't be afraid to stray from the well-trodden paths and seek out the lesser-known treasures. Places like Quy Nhon, the floating markets of the Mekong, or the mountain villages of Ha Giang are perfect examples of how much more there is to discover beyond the popular destinations. These hidden gems often offer a more authentic and intimate experience of Vietnam, and they are well worth the effort to explore. In terms of practical recommendations, preparation is key. Make sure to respect local customs and traditions, as Vietnam is a country rich in culture and history. Familiarize yourself with basic phrases in Vietnamese; a simple greeting in the local language can go a long way in establishing connections with the people you meet. Pack appropriately for the regions you'll be visiting, and always be aware of the local weather, as it can vary significantly depending on where you are in the country. As you plan your trip, remember that Vietnam is not just a destination—it is a journey into the heart of Southeast Asia, where ancient traditions meet modern life. The people of Vietnam, with their open-hearted hospitality, will make you feel welcome, and the landscapes will leave you breathless. But most of all, Vietnam will leave an indelible mark on your soul, changing the way you see the world and offering a new perspective on life.

In closing, I invite you to take that step forward. Let Vietnam captivate you, let it challenge you, and let it inspire you. Whether this is your first trip or one of many, Vietnam is a place that always has something new to offer. Its depth, diversity, and beauty are unmatched, and the memories you create here will stay with you forever. The adventure of a lifetime is waiting for you in Vietnam—are you ready to begin?

Printed in Great Britain
by Amazon